WOMEN IN INDIA
A SEARCH FOR IDENTITY

WOMEN IN INDIA
A SEARCH FOR IDENTITY

Edited by
Dr. (Mrs.) Sharada Rath
Dr. (Mrs.) Navaneeta Rath

ANMOL PUBLICATIONS PVT. LTD.
NEW DELHI - 110 002 (INDIA)

ANMOL PUBLICATIONS PVT. LTD.
4374/4B, Ansari Road, Daryaganj
New Delhi - 110 002

Women in India: A Search for Identity

First Edition, 1999
ISBN 81-261-0450-3

PRINTED IN INDIA

Published by J.L. Kumar for Anmol Publications Pvt. Ltd., New Delhi - 110 002 and Printed at Mehra Offset Press, Delhi.

Contents

Preface

Where do women stand today? What is their identity? Are they "secondary" or "inferior" to the male folk of the society? These are some of the basic questions, which confront the academicians, policy-makers, planners and social activists even during the last part of the 20th century not only in the Third World countries, but also in the western developed countries. It has been, no doubt, a fact that the principle of coexistence and a genuine accommodation has no where been so consciously or unconsciously ignored as in case of women.

Women, world-wide, in fact, contribute more than half of the wealth of nations and yet they are denied economic, social and even legal rights and privileges that such a contribution often entitles men to. The Human Development Report for 1995 published by UNDP presents a gloomy picture on the status of women in the world. The most striking point, the report has made is that there is not a single country where women enjoy equality with men. Women perform $11 trillion worth of unpaid or 'invisible' economic activity world-wide. According to the findings of a 31 - country study, women work longer hours than men. On an average women put in 13 percent more time than men in developed countries. Another finding is that, in developing countries women carry 53 percent and men 47 percent of the total burden of work, while the figures are 51 percent and 49 percent for developed countries. In Nairobi Conference held at the end of the International Women's Decade, it was however, pointed out that still women do two-thirds of world's work but receive only one-tenth of the world's income and own less than one percent of the property.

Coming to India, it can be said that women's search for self and their struggle for survival have had a long chequered history. However, this search has met with two contradictions. One contradiction, we find that while India is a leading country to provide women elite in different periods of history, it is the same country, which stands at the top so far as illiteracy, backwardness and torture of women is concerned. Indian women during the Vedic period enjoyed equal status with men and they were considered as valuable social components for the enrichment of the society. During the Freedom Movement, Indian history is replete with several examples of women of great spirit, valour and battle abilities. Further, in the post-independence period, India could give a woman as the Prime minister to rule the country for more than a decade. But the number of such women during all these periods is very few and the contradiction is that the largest number of women are still being discriminated and subjugated to male dominance in society. Their merits, efficiency, capability and potentialities are being unutilized and wasted on a misconception of their inferior status in society.

The second contradiction is that there exists a great gap between the conceptual role of women in society and their real position and performance since the ancient times of India. "Both (men and women) are God's gifts. They have an equal right to live, and are equally necessary to keep the world going", so said Gandhiji. At the inaugural session of the Ministerial Meeting of the South Asian Association for Regional Cooperation of Women and Development, in Shillong, Mr. Rajiv Gandhi realising the ideological role of women in our society said, "Women and the place of women in society has become a problem in most of our countries. Theoretically, in our country, women have a place of honour, great respect, but there is tremendous difference between the ideal, the aspirations and the reality and practice. As we see it today, women are discriminated against at every stage. Poverty and illiteracy increase this burden. Some segments of women in the middle classes are better off because they have access to education, urbanization and changing social norms. But still the accomplishment is very small."

Even if constitutional provisions relating to gender equality and especially for the development of women have been provided by the Constitution and a number of laws are enacted accordingly, our womenfolk are still searching their self and survival. They still have been subjugated to repression, marginalisation and exploitation for centuries together. It is a shame that in the later part of the 20th century, in India, the tradition of Sati is reviving with the incidence of Roop Kanwar and the atrocities like the "tandoor" incidents are occurring. Wife beating is still, a past time and the incidence of bride burning is on the increase. According to the latest UNDP Report, our Human Development Index (HDI) is 134 among 174 nations. In the case of the status of woman, India's Gender-related Development Index (GDI) is 99 among 130 countries. Such a situational analysis induces the scholars of gender studies to search for the proper self and identity of women in India.

Search for identity of women in India as a movement has gathered momentum particularly in the post-independence period. Several factors may be cited as responsible for such a movement.

First, in India, the Gandhian concept about women in society is still alive, that is, women are a great power in society, but if they misuse their power, it can shatter to bits the whole fabric of society. Second, the constitutional provisions and legal enactment relating to the equality and rights of women make the movement of the search for identity viable. Third, shift from viewing women as target of welfare policies to their empowerment as the critical agent for development and change make the movement possible. Fourth, the effort to relate the women and development debate with the feminist movement is also a causal factor for such a movement. Fifth, in post-independent India, changes have become more pronounced as a result of constitutional provisions, planned economic development, urbanization, industrialization, revolution in science and technology and women cannot be silenced as passive observers of such rapid changes. Finally, exposure of women to formal education and participation in paid labour force are the two key modernization forces which provide interest for the search for women's identity in India.

Women are considered as 'inferior' and 'subservient' to male persons not only in India but world over. A global perspective of the status of women has been discussed by Dr. Brahmananda Satpathy and Jyotirmati Samantray in their article on "Status of Women: A Global Perspective". The authors had given the views of many philosophers, both western and oriental, on women and also tried to analyse the impact of customs, traditions, and religions of different places and of different ages on the status of women. The authors had pointed out that till the end of the first half of the present century, women were considered as inferior to men throughout the world. Sex discrimination was a common phenomenon both in developed as well as developing countries. But the process of decolonisation and the emergence of the two World Wars had changed the picture. Women in every country came forward to join the movement for independence of the colonies. The second half of the century visualised the active participation of women in movements for claiming their rights, identity, freedom, and development throughout the world. Women's issue has not been confined only to one country, but it has become a world-wide phenomenon having global dimensions. There is still a persistent gap between theory and practice for providing rights, equality, and freedom to women everywhere in the world, and this is also the case in india.

Dr. Harihar Mishra in his article titled, "Manu Misunderstood: A Fresh Look at His Attitude Towards Women" has challenged those feminists and other activists who misinterpret Manusmruti and criticise Manu as against the liberation of women and equal status of women with that of men in society. Dr. Mishra, throughout his discussion interprets the writings of Manu and concludes that though Manu had upheld the idea of dependence of women on male persons, but he always gave high status to women as creation starts with women.

The status of women in India, past and present, has been discussed by Dr. (Mrs.) Navaneeta Rath in her article "Women's Identity in India: past and present" as well as by Dr. R. Veermani and T. Ravi in their joint article titled "Women in Indian Society : Prospects and Perceptions". Dr. Navaneeta Rath, in her critical analysis, tried to point out that women, since ancient times, are enjoying a position which is not static through all ages, but is changing very often with the changes of social mores and traditions. Therefore, while women in ancient India had enjoyed a status of equality based on the concept of Shiva and Shakti, in middle ages, they enjoyed a status of subjugation and subordination based on the concept of women as appendages to males in society. Again, in the pre-independence period, women's emancipation started at the call of Mahatma Gandhi, Swami Vivekananda, Raja Rammohan Roy and other freedom fighters. The Freedom Fighters realised that India's independence had been tagged with the full participation of all the people of India- both male and female in the non-violence and non-cooperation movement. Independence of the country, constitution-making, social legislation and governmental programmes, however have changed the status of women in a more progressive way. In a similar tone, Dr. R. Veeramani and T. Ravi had argued in their article that women's status could be progressively changed, had they been properly educated. To them, women must realize their capabilities and proper opportunities should be given to them for utilizing their potentialities. So, though women accept a job for economic benefits, self-expression should be the motivating factor for joining a paid job. In author's view this would give an equal status to women in society.

Legislation is the mechanism through which social objectives are to be achieved. Women have searched their proper identity, equality and empowerment through various social enactments. Dr. S.C. Jena , in his paper on "Women and Social Legislation in India" has discussed various social laws which were enacted from time to time in India with a purpose to elevate women's status in society. In his paper, the author has made an elaborate discussion of the constitutional provisions relating to women's equality, rights and privileges as well as the social laws which were enacted during the pre-independence as well as post-independence India. The author tries to make an assessment of all these laws in operation and points out the lacunae in these laws, so far as the objectives for achieving gender-equality is concerned. The author concludes that the legal provisions have proved of limited help. The rights created by legal provisions have been treated as ends in themselves instead of means. The similar view has been expressed by Dr. (Mrs) Navaneeta Rath in her second article titled "Identity Search for Women in India And Legislation". The author discusses various important laws enacted specifically for giving proper status, identity, equality and independence to women in society. These laws may be categorised as social, educational, economic and political. The author points out that India is the most unique country where women possess numerous and important rights for their self-assertion as a reflection of their identity in society. But there is a wide gap between the theory and practice. The real scenario differs much from the prescribed one. The laws have not yet achieved reasonable success, so far as emancipation, equality, empowerment and search for identity of women in India are concerned.

The problems and issues of rural women are certainly different from those of urban women in general. This has been discussed by Dr. (Mrs.) Sharada Rath, who had viewed in her article that women's development in India can be perceived from a grassroots development perspective. The author has argued that any development policies for rural women in India are to be construed taking into consideration their specific needs and problems and their potentialities.

The role of mass media in searching for proper identity of women in modern society has been discussed by Dr. (Mrs.) Madhusmita Misra in her paper titled "Women and Media:The Indian Scenario". Dr. Misra had pointed out that in modern society media have got two important roles, so far as women's problems are concerned. These roles are, namely to create mass awareness by portraying women in their proper position, their needs and claims as well as the expected role of women in family, community and in society as a whole. Secondly, mass media have got an important role to inculcate the values, beliefs and orientations of women towards the polity and society in the minds of women. So, women can be aware of their rights, duties and responsibilities not only for the family but as active citizens for the nation. However, Dr. Misra has concluded that so far as women's problems and their awareness are concerned, Indian media have not yet performed their roles properly.

Anil Dutta Misra in his paper titled "Communalism and Women" has discussed the concept of communalism and its relationship with women's issues. In his study, he has made it clear that there are two factors, namely, gender and religion, which are responsible for lowering the interests, integrity and identity of women in India. In India, since independence, debates on communalism, fundamentalism and religious revivalism are always linked with the question of women's issues and because of the present political culture, women always become the prey of foul power politics. The author establishes this fact with argument that communal organisations curtail women's fundamental rights and communal tensions, riots and violence create dangers for women's survival and freedom.

H.Nageswar Rao in his paper titled, "Kamma Political Elites in Andhra Pradesh and Women's Equal Right to Property" has made a study on the attitude of Kamma political elites in general and Panchayat Samithi Presidents in particular towards the movement on the issue of women's equal right to property. The author, in this empirical study, has made an analysis of different factors for which there was the support for the movement as well as the opposition for the movement. However, he concludes that when the leaders remain indifferent to lend support to such a constitutional and legal issue, it is difficult to create a society based on gender equality.

Participation in economic field is crucial to women's struggle for a better social status. This has been discussed in the paper titled "Women and Their Work Environment" written by Dr (Mrs) Swarnamayee Tripathy. The author made an empirical study of the attitude and perception of women towards their work environment. The author points out that the advent of industrialisation, introduction of western education, intrusion of modern values and the working of the Constitution of India have brought significant changes in the lives of women in India, so far as job opportunities and work environment are concerned. Despite these changes, women workers as yet, do not constitute a homogenous social class. The study reveals that the women workers are mostly engaged in low-paid jobs and they have very little knowledge about their constitutional and legal rights, for which they are being victimised and discriminated in their work place. The author concludes that women's right to organise and struggle against their oppression must be linked with the question of the democratic rights of the people.

However, political participation is preceded by awareness of political values and objects, which an individual gets through a process of learning known as political socialisation. The agencies and extent of political socialisation of working women have thus been discussed in the paper on "Political Socialisation of Working Women" written jointly by Dr. (Mrs.) Sharada Rath and Ms.Gayatri Kar. The authors' findings state that the awareness of working women regarding political personalities and political parties are adequate, but their knowledge about legal provisions for women is not adequate. Moreover, there is a positive relationship between the education and awareness of working women. So far as agencies of political socialisation are concerned, it is found that mass media influence most in socialising working women in general.

. Political participation of women is one of the major indicators of women's status and identity. Women are supposed to be not only the subjects but also the participants in the decision-making bodies of the country. The authors who have seen the problems from various angles and have analysed the problem of low participation of women in the political process have discussed this. Ms. Jayashree Tripathy, in her paper on "Women in Indian Politics" gives a historical sketch of women's entry and involvement in Indian politics from the pre-independence period to date. She has indicated the limits of women's role in politics and to her, political activism is still regarded as male's domain to which women's entry is few and far between. She concludes that, the women's issue, if it is to be resolved by equality of rights and responsibilities, is basically a political one which needs the political involvement and activism of women themselves. The following three other articles deal with the political participation of women at micro level.

Dr.Ramesh Chandra Mishra has made an in-depth study of the representation, role performance, and role- perception of women legislators of Orissa State Assembly. Despite the constitutional promise of a political atmosphere free from discrimination of any kind, there exists gender discrimination legally invisible though, in the realm of politics, largely because of the continuation of the in-built inhibitions of the Indian patriarchal society. To the author, politics has traditionally been viewed as a male preserve. Women representation in Orissa Assembly is very low and their socio-economic status largely influences the role-perception of women legislators. The author proves that in the Orissa Assembly, women members believe protecting and promoting popular interests as to be the ultimate aim of their legislative functions. Most of the women legislators perceived the interests of the constituents to be inclusive of the women interests. Though, women legislators feel that they have some women- interest role to play, they have not been able to identify themselves with problems that affect women specifically.

Dr. Urmimala Das, in her article, "Aetiology of Gender Gap in Political Representation of Orissa" has narrated the causes for which women representation in decision-making process is very low. Even if women constitute 49% of the total population, the women representatives in Orissa Assembly count only 3.4% in average. The number of female members in the Cabinet and Council of Ministers is also very marginal. The author points out that even these women representatives represent more the general cause than the female cause, as they win the election because of their integration with existing male system and not due to their fight for women's cause. No political party has yet developed confidence in the capability of women and it never gives any chance to women to show their merit, capability and efficiency in the political decision-making body. The author concludes that in order to achieve a decisive role in politics, women must be aware of power and their interests. Women must be convinced that there can be no better advocates of their interests than themselves.

Mrs. Mandakini Das in her paper titled "Women's Participation in Electoral Politics: A Study of the Dhenkanal Assembly Constituency of Orissa", speaks of the political participation of women as candidates from Dhenkanal constituency in Assembly elections in Orissa. In her study, the author points out that this constituency always supports a lady candidate in every Assembly election. On the contrary, the author concludes that victory of lady candidate in the election in this constituency is purely a personal factor and it does not prove the high rate of awareness, interest, and involvement of women as a group in the electoral process.

Women all over the world have got their rights, equality and empowerment through movements with different issues and patterns. This has been discussed in the paper on "Women's Movement: A Crave for Gender Equality", written by Dr. (Mrs.) Sharada Rath and Mrs. Jyotirmati Samantray. The authors have put forth that, in India, feminism is not understood as radical feminism of the west, but it is identified with the terms like "women's liberation", "women's emancipation", "women's uplift", and "women's equality". Though women's movement in India has started as a part of the National Movement for a common cause, that is, independence of the country, but it proved successful for sensitization and mobilization of women for understanding their own problems. Through agitation, women started for struggling to achieve their demands for equality, rights, development and empowerment. The authors conclude that the issues and dimensions of women's movement in India have become more broad-based and the movement pattern has been perceivably changed at the end of this century

Keeping all these viewpoints in mind, the present work is a collection of selected essays emphasising on the changing identity of women in social, political and economic arena in both pre-independence and post-independence India. Some of these papers were presented in different seminars and conferences and some of the papers are written in gist form from the research work of the authors for academic degrees. We are sure that the papers we have selected for inclusion in this book would give the readers an insight to the issue of women's identity in society, politics, employment and in movements. We hope that the expositions outlined will be found quite useful by social science researchers, policy-makers, planners and social activists who are working in the area of women's development and empowerment.

SHARADA RATH
NAVANEETA RATH

Our Contributors

Anil Dutta Misra, M.A., Assistant Professor, Department of Non-Violence and Peace Research, Jain Vishva Bharati Institute, Ladnun- 341306, Rajasthan.

Brahmananda Satpathy, Ph.D. Reader in Political Science, Utkal University, Bhubaneswar, Orissa.

Gayatri Kar, Ph.D.Research Scholar, Department of Political Science, Utkal University.

H. Nageswar Rao, Department of Political Science, Osmania University, Hyderabad.

Harihar Mishra, Ph.D. Controller of Examinations, Sri Jagannath Sanskrit University, Sri Vihar, Puri, Orissa.

Jayashree Tripathy, O.F.S. Assistant Commercial Tax Officer, Puri, Orissa.

Jyotirmati Samantaray, Assistant Information Officer, Soochana Bhawan, Government of Orissa.

Madhusmita Mishra, Ph.D., Post-Doctoral Scholar, Department of Political Science, Utka University, Bhubaneswar, Orissa.

Mandakini Das, Lecturer in Political Science, G.M.College, Sambalpur, Orissa.

Navaneeta Rath, Ph.D., Lecturer in Sociology, R. D.Women's College,Bhubaneswar.

R.Veeramani, Ph.D. Lecturer in Economics, ICE, University of Madras.

Ramesh Chandra Mishra, Department of Political Science, S.C.S. College, Puri, Orissa.

Sharada Rath, Ph.D., Professor of Political Science, Utkal University, Bhubaneswar.

Sudhir Ch. Jena, Ph.D. Senior Lecturer in Political Science, F.M. College, Balasore.

Swarnamayee Tripathy, Ph.D., Lecturer in Political Science, Paradeep College, Paradeep, Orissa.

T. Ravi, M.A., Research Scholar, Department of Economics, ICE, University of Madras.

Urmi Mala Das, Research Associate, Center for Women Studies, Berhampur University, Bhanj Vihar, Berhampur, Ganjam, Orissa.

1

STATUS OF WOMEN: A GLOBAL PERSPECTIVE

Dr. Brahmananda Satapathy
Jyotirmati Samantray

Simon de Beauvoir has described women as "The Second Sex". Women have been attributed a second nature and glorified for their unique capacity for patience, for suffering, for unselfishness and the ability to submerge their personality for the common good of the family.

Women however, have been glorified for wrong reasons—to perpetuate their suppression and elevate the hold of the patriarchal society to retain the dominance of men over them. The commonly held belief that women have greater patience and forbearance is shared by all alike, the educated and uneducated, oriental as well as accidentals. This unanimously held view of the "characteristic virtue of women" held to be inherent in the sex as a whole is imposed on all women until it becomes the universally accepted viewpoint.

The process of "de-individualisation" starts as soon as girls are born. Most of them are not allowed to develop a personality of their own. Right from her birth a woman experiences her inferiority, dependence bondage, till all these become a part of her.[1] Smt. G. Suvarna Rani, in her article "Empowerment of Women", points out that, just as the "Percolation theory" failed, so also equal distribution of benefits between men and women failed. The reason is that certain socio-cultural factors held women chained preventing them from accessing all the institutions and agencies set up for development. This has resulted in polarisation of all the benefits towards men.

In his edited book titled, *The Potential of Women*, Seymour M. Farber and Roger H.L. Wilson explained that, the simple dichotomy of "innate" *vs.* "acquired" is conceptually outdated in analysis of developmental differentiation of femininity and masculinity, which is not to say that one should obliterate the distinction between genetics and environment. World Bank Development Report (1991) concludes that economic success for women will improve their own lives and those of all Indians. For this end, women's access to goods and services, to productive assets and to factory and markets must be improved and brought probably at par with that of Indian males.[2]

The process of underdevelopment and the connections of present developmental efforts to international capitalist system have profound significance for women. Eastor Boserup's pioneering work, *Women and Development* (1970), first drew attention to the special and particular ways in which these changes over the last couple of centuries were affecting the lives of women – the ways in which they affected women in each country depended much on the prevailing social structure.

Real development would mean ending a system, which increases the gap between rich and poor nations. The improvement of the status of women requires a change in the attitudes and roles of both men and women. Women's development should not only be viewed as an issue in social development but should be seen as an essential component in every dimensions of development. To improve the status of women and their role in the process of development, such development should be an integral part of global project for the establishment of a New International Economic Order based on equity, sovereign equality, interdependence, common interest and co-operation among all the nation-states.[3]

A high level World Bank team, put the gender-related issues to the fore to ensure that the adverse impact of structural adjustment and stabilisation of the economy did not fall squarely on activities concerning women and child welfare, health, education and family welfare,[4] despite their contributions in various fields, very little has been done or given to encourage women to emerge from the stereo-typed role assigned to them in society.

Women across the world have, after years of struggle, been able to achieve the right to vote. They now make up more than half of most electorates, and many more women work in the public sector than even before. Is it not surprising and disturbing that despite all their qualities and capabilities women rarely achieve elective office or have equal access to political careers? They are blocked from top positions in trade unions, political parties, government, interested associations and business. The triumphant march of democracy in all parts of the globe has aroused the collective conscience of the people to shed regimentation and unleash forces that have liberating influence in society, polity and economy. It is this anchoring of modern day life on democracy and the increasing exertion for equal rights for both men and women that have paved the way for according top priority to women's issues in the global agenda.

Despite the pressures of society and systems, women have in different periods of history, emerged to the forefront and proved their mettle. Queen Victoria of England, Margaret Thatcher, Zenobia, Razia Sultan and Rani Laxmi Bai of Jhansi to our late Prime Minister Indira Gandhi are but a few names in the galaxy of women leaders who have left an indelible mark on the pages of world history.

The fact remains that despite being denied their due rights in the society, women have formed the bedrock of stability. In today's world as in the past, women form the cohesive factor in a society affected by ethnic, political and economic and religious pulls and pressures. The great poet philosopher Khalil Gibran pays tribute to the women in the following words: "Women opened the windows of my eyes and doors of my spirit. Had it not been for the woman-mother, the woman sister and the woman friend, I would have sleeping among those who seek the tranquillity of the world with their snoring."

However, women constituting half of the world population and contributing to two-thirds of human activity, have remained relegated to the secondary status as far as the enjoyment of their rights are concerned. The oppressive conditions within which they grow up the countervailing forces they confront and the subjective perception they nurture do not induce them to play a meaningful role in the society. This attitude is indeed a restricting factor in the individual's growth. The saying of the French writer, Simon de Beauvoir is very much correct that "when an individual is kept in a situation of inferiority, the fact is that he does become inferior." This tendency has to be negated and at times reversed to conjure up a better vision for the fair sex.[5]

It is difficult to specify a correct methodology for community-based approaches to women's issues. The process of mobilisation and conscientisation, which attempts to make women aware of the problems, challenges and choices cannot be external. The reason is that it involves both a subjective understanding of the elements of oppression and an objective decision to transform their realities by building their capacities for participation, and self-development, short-term campaigns, do little to change attitude but to focus attention on specific issues. The process has to be continuous and should provide a common basis or framework for both an understanding and analysis of manifest problems, and possible collective action, if the goals are comprehensive to the community and the efforts do not seem far ahead of women's consciousness.[6]

The development of a nation can not only be measured through the technological and materialistic advances, but through the quality of life people live. The growth of a nation lies in its capacity to elevate the lot of the weakest sections of the society. In this sense, women constitute the weakest section of the society, as they are least empowered. Pandit Jawaharlal Nehru had rightly stated: "The status of women indicates the character of a country".[7] What do we mean by "status"? Status is a composite concept, which indicates the position of an individual or group in terms of several values in society. Status may be analysed in terms of the extent to which a person is perceived to receive rewards and incur costs as well as with the extent of his/her investment, his/her past history or background.[8]

Functioning of societies depends upon the presence of patterns for reciprocal behaviour between individuals or groups of individuals. The polar position in such patterns of reciprocal behaviour is technically known as statuses. The term 'status' like the term 'culture' has come to be used with a double significance. A 'status' in the abstract, is a position in a particular pattern. It represents individual's position in relation to the whole society. A role represents the dynamic aspect of status. Societies have met the dilemmas by developing two types of statuses, the 'ascribed' and the 'achieved'. Ascribed statuses are those which are assigned to individuals without reference to their innate differences or abilities. The achieved statuses as a minimum are those requiring special qualities, although they are not necessarily limited to these.

Any attempt to assess the status of women in a society should ideally start from the social framework. Social structure, cultural norms and value systems are important determinants of women's roles and their position in society.[9] However, women, all over the world, fare worse than the male on the scale of development, which relegates them to a position of inferior status. The only difference between women from the developed and developing countries lies in the nature of gender deprivations and discrimination suffered. Life-style and consumption patterns may be almost as par between men and women in the developed world. In case of less developed countries like India even these may be denied to women, which is not to speak of compounding deprivation that may follow from the very denial of these basic necessities. It appears that while women's issues in the developed world are more sharply focussed on the equality question, in the Third World countries, the issues are seen primarily as developmental.[10]

The debate as to whether the genesis of women's subordination and marginalisation lies in the sexual division of labour, or in social stratification and the emergence of exploitative structures remains inconclusive. The women's liberation movement in the West has however, pushed to the forefront many other issues relating to women's oppression and discrimination. The subjugation of women has become a universal phenomenon and it is more or less present in all cultures and societies. The relationship between the population dimensions of development and roles and status of women and how they get reflected in the dynamics of social attitudes and public policies is just the beginning to be explored. One can however, say that this issue cannot be examined in isolation but must necessarily take note of the cultural, the economic, the structural and political dimensions of the whole process of social transformations.

While women's roles and status are central to most of the discussions, there is no consensus on what are the basic dimensions of women's status. Are there some universal factors, which determine women's position in different cultures and can provide a comparative perspective? Is women's position determined by cultural values, economic system, social and politico-legal structures or ideological superstructures (religion, customs and tradition)? How do women visualise their roles and the determinants of status within various systems and subsystems i.e. family, community and the wider society and perceive the origin and instruments of their oppression? How do women form their identity, self-image and value systems?

The indicators of women's status may be grouped as follows:

1. Female infant mortality rate
2. Maternal mortality
3. Female literacy rate
4. Women's age at marriage
5. Sex ratio
6. Status of female child in the family and society
7. Employment status of women
8. Property rights of women
9. Participation of women in the political, economic and social life of the country
10. Incidence of social evils, such as Sati, divorce, domestic accidents, rape, dowry deaths etc., and
11. Social and personal oppression of women.

Along with the above indicators, several methods have also been used in assessing the status of women in a society.

1. Historical Method

This method focuses on legacy in ancient society and its perpetuation in medieval and present periods. Social scientists draw important conclusions about women's status from the work of historians and philosophers of science. For example, Altekar using the historical method analysed the status of women in ancient India with a careful consideration of their social, economic, political, religious and general status. Neera Desai, later on used this approach to establish the actual manner by which certain perspectives and evidence come to be accepted over others. Even today many sociologists consider historical analysis as a necessary aspect of a holistic approach to the study of changing status of women. However, some scholars believe that simplistic citing of examples from the religious scriptures or available records of the past does not constitute a historical analysis and is really very informative. Sociologists trained in the generally reductionism procedures of the hypothetical-deductive method, and other forms of positivism find it difficult, if not impossible, to study women's status with historical approach.

2. Non-Empirical Case Study Method

Using the non-empirical case study method, the scholars have analysed the status of women in terms of patriarchy as a social system, or relationship between sexual inequality and status of women. The low status of women is explained as the result of dominance of men over women, which has existed historically and cross-culturally.

3. Empirical Method of Assessing Inter-Personal Power

Using the above method, the scholars have studied male domination over women but in isolation from the patriarchal system of which it is a part. It holds that the problem (of low status, exploitation / denial of rights) lies in the dominance over women and the answer lies in the struggle against it. This body of research has focussed not on structured inequality on the societal level but on inequality and the balance of power within the family. The empirical study includes in-depth interviews with women of different communities, classes and categories who have experienced different behaviour from their husbands and in-laws. Empirical method is being used particularly when we make comparative study of the status of women with that of male persons in different dimensions like economic dimension, educational dimension, social dimension, political dimension and legal dimension. In this method, hypotheses are being framed, primary data are collected, categorised, and analysed to verify the hypotheses. Empirical method is being used particularly when we make comparative study of the status of women with that of male persons in different dimensions like economic dimension, educational dimension, social dimension, political dimension and legal dimension. In this method, hypotheses are being framed, primary data are collected, categorised, and analysed to verify the hypotheses.

4. Empirical Quantitative and Qualitative Questionnaire Method

In this method questions are asked to the respondents on selected items pertaining to behaviour, privileges enjoyed and inter-personal relations inside and outside the family. The quantitative data are used for qualitative analysis. Besides the above methods of assessing women's changing status, two scales are suggested for this purpose, such as,

(a) Women's individualisation scale :

* Marriage choice
* Age at marriage
* Money handler
* Range of movement from hearth
* Divorce right

(b) Women's role-status scale :

* Right to vote
* Right to contest for Parliamentary/Assembly elections
* Right to hold governmental posts
* Right to hold diplomatic, judicial and administrative posts
* Right to be treated without any sex discrimination.

IMAGES OF WOMEN IN RELIGIOUS TRADITIONS

In respect of status that is accorded to women by law and by the constitution, we notice that there is a gap between the theoretical possibilities and their actual realisation. Religion, family and kinship, roles and cultural norms delimiting the spheres of women's activities obstruct their full and equal participation in society and the achievement of their full potential.

Religion itself is born and nurtured in a certain type of structure that cannot be denied; nor it can be denied that religion imparts legitimacy and is functional to sustain certain kinds of social structure. It provides ideological and moral bases for the accorded status and institutionalised roles of women in a society. The social restrictions on women and also the people's notions about their proper roles in the domestic and extra-domestic spheres, are largely derived from the religious notions of women's basic characteristics, their assumed 'virtues' and 'vices', their proverbial strengths and weaknesses and the stereotypes regarding their nature and capabilities. Religion has, in fact, a dynamic character and is shaped and reshaped by historical processes through diverse interpretations and value emphasis at the hands of different authorities in different periods of time.

HINDUISM

Hinduism has a long history full of contradictions. During the centuries of its existence, the image of women has undergone many changes. It is said that women in the Vedic period enjoyed a high status. Women in the later ages pictured in the epics, the Puranas and the *Dharmashastra* have travelled a long way and can be seen in some ways even in modern age.

On the other hand, in the same religion, a woman is described by a multitude of derogatory attributes. She is called fickle-minded, sensual, seducer of men; given to falsehood, trickery, folly, greed, impurity and thoughtless action, root of all evil, inconsistent and crucial. There are exhortations that a woman should be kept under control. In childhood she must be subject to her father, in youth to her husband, and when her husband dies to her sons. "A woman must never be independent". This dictum of Manu, the first Hindu law-giver, along with Tulsidas's well-known stanza in which he groups women with drums, morons, *Shudras* and cattle as objects fit to be beaten.

THE BHAKTI MOVEMENT

The Bhakti Movement, which arose during the medieval period denounced complicated rituals, and asserted that God could be worshipped not only through knowledge and rituals but also by devotion. The history of the *Bhakti Movement* reveals that it brought great solace to women and presented an alternative way of life to many individual women.

VEERASAIVISM

Combining work and devotion, Veerasaivism was at the time of its inception, a democratising movement. The corpus of religious love of Veerasaivism consists of 'Vachanas" (sayings) of 200 to 300 saints, of whom about 50 persons were women.

ISLAM

The Islamic religion propagates that man and woman stand on a footing of equality in their relationship with the Divine. Woman like man, is an individual who can pray to the Almighty and can hope for redemption. Islam does not consider woman as an impediment in the path of religion nor does it consider her as the root cause of man's downfall. But, in course of time, this concept of women's equality in Islamic religion has become diluted and the Muslim Shariat Law as developed and practised over the centuries places women in a disadvantageous or an inferior position in many respects.

In Islam, a woman is as much a believer of Almighty, but she cannot be a priest, nor she can lead the prayers. She has no place in the formal religious organisation and legal affairs of the community. She cannot be appointed as a *Kazi*. *The Quran*, the Muslim *Dhamagrantha* emphasises modesty, decorum and chastity only for women. The practice of Talaq or unilateral divorce on the part of only man has made the status of Muslim women very deplorable. Again Muslim women have to lead a life of seclusion and they have no right to participate in communal prayers.

CHRISTIANITY

In India, communities of various denominations represent Christianity. In each of these communities, the practice of the tenets of Christianity has been influenced in varying degrees, by historical as well as by contemporary and by socio-cultural factors.

This has resulted in overshadowing, suppressing or reviving and bringing into focus the essence of teaching of Christianity regarding the status and role of women. Her status is much better than the status of a daughter-in-law in patriarchal families of the upper caste Hindus. The Bible lays great emphasis on the image of a woman as strong and steady influence for the good.

In Christianity, both men and women are believed to have been created by God in his own image. Thus, a woman is as much entitled to strive for her salvation as man. In fact, every other role in her life is subordinated to this role. In Christianity, women have been entitled to study religious scripture and to participate in all religious ceremonies. She has a right to become a nun. Christianity accepts equality between men and women.

JAINISM

As a way of life Jainism lays great stress on self-denial,

restraint of passion, and a life of renunciation, for both men and women. A woman has a legitimate position in the congregational life. By and large, religious learning and renunciation are allowed to woman who has a full right to aspire for *moksha*. However, in the religious context, it can not be ignored that in ascetic manuals and sermons there is severe condemnation of woman who is looked upon as a tempter and seducer and is called tricky, deceptive, hypocrite, fickle, untrustworthy and treacherous. Although, actual customs and practices of the Jains often depend on their environmental setting and thus manifest differences between north and south, east and west. Certain basic features of the faith have definite influence on the status of woman. In the context of the family, chastity in women is greatly valued and several stories in Jain scriptures are woven round this theme.

BUDDHISM

Buddhism recognised broad parity between man and woman in matters of religion, both the sexes being charged alike with the duty of upholding Dharma. Buddhism as a liberal reaction against orthodox *Brahminism* elevated the status of women. Buddhism does not consider women as evil or as one solely responsible for sensuality in the world. In Ladakh, and other parts of India, where Buddhist people are found, women enjoy some sort of equality with men, particularly in relation to religious rites and performance.

SIKHISM

Sikhism condemns formal rituals, idolatry and superstition. It emphasises simple devotion to God. In the pursuit of religion, both men and women have a place as individuals. Sikhism looks at woman as man's helpmate and sharer in his domestic life and she should be respected. It does not look upon woman as an agent of sin and evil, nor does it regard her as an object of pleasure. For the purpose of devotion, there is no difference between man and woman. In social life, however, Sikhism did not concede equality for women.

ZOROSTRIANISM

In India, there are less than 1,00,000 Parsees, who follow Zorostrianism, one of the oldest religions of the world. Zorostrian women enjoy a position of honour in the family and in society. They are entitled to both religious and secular education.

WESTERN PHILOSOPHERS ON THE STATUS OF WOMEN

It is true that the early Western Philosophers were more concerned about the State and its unity than about the women's status, role or position. Keeping the state on a higher plane, Plato advocated "communism of family" and "communism of property" not from any feminist point of view, but for providing good rulers for good states. His theory of "communism of family" is based on logical deductions for establishing an ideal state.

Aristotle had never considered women as best citizens and they were considered as inferior to men. So, women needed to be controlled by the male persons. They were meant only for procreation purpose - man provided the 'form' and the woman provided the 'matter'. Aristotle had taken man as the 'natural' ruler and women were subservient to men. This theory of Aristotle was based upon alleged natural differences.

However, the philosophers of Natural Law School advocated for equality of men and women. Hobbes insisted that paternal power in the State of Nature be not derived from fatherhood as such. If patriarchal sovereignty was a product of procreation, then the mother, who is a full partner in the act of generation, should have an equal claim on the child. Locke assumed that familial authority belonged to the mother as much as to the father. Parents have a joint dominion over their children. Mother specially has a great share in nourishing the child. Rousseau holds that all men and women are created equal. He argues that woman's sharply distinct position is due to those characteristics that are natural to her sex. Her procreative faculties make her unlike man who has been categorised in terms of a generally limitless potential, rational, tough and creative. Woman has been described as soft, modest and simple. He believed that in endowing fair sex with certain compensations, like the gift of coquetries, nature has ensured that woman does not become the slave of man. Rather, an average woman can manage very well by preserving her natural coquetries at various levels of behaviour. In fact, he gave a long list of "feminine qualities" for women.

Coming to Utilitarian School, it is found that Bentham, who advocated for "greatest happiness of the greatest number", universal suffrage and secret ballot, was a covert feminist. According to him, sensibility of woman is greater than that of man, but she is inferior to him in physical strength. She is fit for family life and man for the outside life. But this does not mean that woman is altogether excluded from public sphere. In the same line, John Stuart Mill propounded that one of the principal purposes of societal and political institutions was to develop human potential to the highest possible stage. The emancipation of women to a level of equality with men was not for Mill aimed solely at the happiness of women themselves though it was an important part of it. It was a prerequisite for the improvement of mankind. Liberty and self-determination are the recurrent themes of Mill's argument against the gross inequality of the marriage laws and severe discrimination suffered by women in the areas of educational and occupational opportunity. He advocated for emancipation of women and severely criticised the doctrine of inferiority, which had been greatly supported by Aristotle and Rousseau.

According to the Socialist School of thinkers the gender inequality prevails in a capitalist society, because by marriage, wife becomes the private property of man. In early stages of society, women became the subordinate wives when the development of valuable productive resources, initially in the form of domestication of large animals as private property started. Technology changed the relations between men and women within the "household" as the family overshadowed the clan as the key economic and decision-making group. As the nature of the "household" changed, significance of women's work and her position in the society deteriorated. Women now work for their husbands instead of the society.[11]

In Indian political philosophy, women were originally considered as equal, because they were the equal creation of God and they were thought to be equal parts of Nature. Manu, the first Hindu law-giver, however, provided a subordinate position to women because of their biological necessity. According to Manu, woman needs help from man at every stage of her life. But, in the 19th century and onwards, the Indian political thinkers advocated for equal rights, privileges and equal social status of man and woman.

GENDER INEQUALITY: A GLOBAL VIEW

Women, throughout the world are considered as inferior, subordinate and subject to discrimination. This has been supported by many proverbial statements. For example, in Russia, there is an old proverb that there is only one soul among ten women. The Spaniards say, "We shall save ourselves from wicked women, and should never be captivated by any that has good look." The Italian proverb goes a step further and pronounces, "as a horse whether good or bad require spurs, so a woman, whether good or bad, requires thrashing." In India also, the proverb goes that if one will listen to woman's advice, he will be ruined.

In fact, at present, all these proverbs relating to inferior status of women have become meaningless. All over the world, there have been a lot of movements, agitations and legislations to improve the status of women and to make them equal with the male persons of the society. In many countries, the struggle for freedom from colonial rule provided scope for women development. Women leaders in India, Burma, Indonesia, Vietnam etc. ably demonstrated their capabilities as fellow fighters in the nationalist movements. The Congress, which was fighting for independence of India, accepted the principle of gender equality through its Fundamental Rights Resolution adopted in Karachi Session in 1931. These national movements resulted not only making the nation free, but also in emancipation of women. In some of the newly emergent African States, for example, Samoa, the Constitution provides equal political rights to both the sexes.

A survey conducted by an independent agency, Population Quisiz Committee (1988) indicates that despite the emancipation of women in the present time, the status of women in no country is good. It is relatively best in Sweden, second in order are Finland and America. Afghanistan occupies the last position, while Pakistan, Iraq, Algeria, Libya, Saudi Arab and North Yemen occupy the bottom position. A recent survey conducted in U.S.A. (1992) by National Victim Center shows that 61% of the rape victims are girls of less than 11 years. Similarly, in about 78% of the cases the rapists are either relatives or intimates of the victims.

In Socialist countries, women occupy relatively a better social position, but in politics, their role is minimal. In the erstwhile Soviet Union, although the Supreme Soviet had many women members, they were totally absent from the Politburo and they comprised less than four per cent of the total membership of CPSU. Similar is the case in China. In 1965, no woman served in the Politburo, while only four served on the Eighth CCP Committee. This has been well illustrated in a document prepared by the UN Social and

Economic Council in 1967. New Zealand was the first country & the world to extend voting right to women in 1893, but it took forty years for them to be elected to its House of Representatives. Another remarkable feature is that in the 60's and 70's the number of women representatives in popular House in many countries declined. In U.S.A., for example, the number of women in the House of Representatives was 18 in 1964, but it came down in 1972. Similarly, in West Germany the number declined from 48 in 1957 to 33 in 1969. In France, the number of women representatives from 40 in 1946 came down to 11 in 1967. In Asian countries however, the declining trend was not so apparent. In both Sri Lanka and Phillippines, there were only one lady member in their Parliament in 1947 and 1952, which became six after the 1972 elections. In Japan, 34 women were elected in 1946, but the number came down to 7 in 1972. In India, the number of women elected to Lok Sabha had remained fluctuating from 22 in 1952, to 44 in 1984.

In the light of the above discussion, the following points emerge:

1. That inequality in status of male and female is a global phenomenon. Women are adversely treated and are subjected to discrimination on ground of their sex.
2. That the magnitude of discrimination and mal-treatment to women, however, varies in different countries and in different parts (or societies) of the same country.
3. That there has been a global concern against the discrimination and mal-treatment of women which has manifested itself in organised movements, agitations and adoption of legislations in many countries.
4. That on account of growing concern for education, economic independence and measures adopted, the

gap between the two sexes has narrowed almost through out the world.[12]

FEMINISM AND IDEOLOGY

Feminism is marching ahead since International Women's Decade. Broadly speaking, the essential idea of feminism is the equality of woman with man. But, there are two schools of feminists. One school asserts that women are in no way inferior to men and they are of equal worth. They put emphasis on gender equality. The other school claims for women not a position of equality with men, but one of superiority. The feminist idea understood in the above terms is undeniably the product of ideas about the nature of man and about the ethical basis of his relations in society.[13]

The feminists speak of two approaches to deal with the problems of women development. These approaches are (1) Moderate or Liberal Feminism, and (2) Radical or Marxist Feminism and both are found in women's liberation movement which is spreading in different forms and intensity in all parts of the world. The adherents of the radical approach believe that revolution is necessary to liberate women ant to make them equal with men. Moderate feminists, on the other hand, do not find it necessary to resort to any type of revolution to improve the condition of women. They believe in social reform and change of social values and attitudes of both men and women in order to bring development of women in society. In India, radical and socialist feminist groups are relatively of recent origin and they are few and scattered far and wide. No moderate feminists have systematically developed a theory of the status of women. Theirs are ad hoc writings on the position of women and their roles and functions. In course of time, the activities of Moderates have changed. The moderates of the U.S.A. and Britain of the twentieth century have adopted relatively more militant postures in comparison to their predecessors of the last century for securing equal rights for women.

Moderate feminist activities are now more than two centuries old. They began with the French Revolution, which gave currency to the areas of liberty, equality, fraternity. The moderate feminism believes in gender equality, that is equal rights to men and women. It rejects subordination of one sex by the other, or treating women as sex objects instead of as human beings. However, this ideology does not challenge the division of labour on sex basis. It holds that woman is best suited for family roles and man for outside roles. The liberal feminists demand genuine equality of opportunity, recognising that women must compete with men in the job market. Their goal is competitive society. They reject sexual division of labour in favour of access to jobs on the basis of merit. They want that domestic necessities may be fulfilled through the market, supplemented via the welfare state, shared between partners (i.e. husband and wife) and minimised by technology. Their commitment to ideals of personal responsibility and autonomy has also drawn them into political support for legal abortion, in order that women might control their own fertility and hence, life choices.

In India, moderate feminism began with the social reform movement. Raja Rammohan Roy protested against many evil social customs like *Sati* in the early 19th century. All social reformers in India, during this period protested against unjust social customs, which led to the subjugated conditions of women. Many, but not all, believed that women should be considered to be 'equal' to man. But, their concept of 'equality' was within the framework of Hindu religious texts. It was the belief that there must be separation of the roles between the sexes, though no 'role' was considered to be superior to the other. According to them, the primary role of a woman was to be a housewife and mother. In fact, in the post-independence period, the moderate feminist activists of India have changed their strategy to some extent to gain women's equality and development in society.[14]

Marxist feminism marks a departure from an earlier

ideology, which rejected feminism as bourgeois. Marx's definition of the proletariat as a privileged and universal class with a historical mission inevitably marginalised an interest in women. Engels' approach in explaining women's oppression as an historical effect of property world over has also been considerably refined today. Engels held that female subordination is the result of emergence of private property and ownership of means of production. The Marxists now hold that female subordination is not limited to propertied male's need for legitimate heirs.

The ideology of radical feminism, though believes in sexual inequality but it rejects traditional division of labour. It holds that the gender roles are the result of biological factors but are the product of culture. It believes in free sex and collective child-care. Thus, when in the nineteenth century, Marxists gave a deterministic orientation to discussions of the woman question that women's oppression is specific to a capitalist mode of production, now Marxists give a more humanistic explanation. Current radical feminism emerged out of the New Left and the student movements of the 1960s. The interest of Cultural Revolution has been reinforced by intellectual developments. In 1980s, Marxist feminism inclined more towards radical variety, which emphasized symbolic rather than material factors, of sexual oppression and which presents the cultural generation of gender (feminine/masculine) personalities. At the ideological level, feminists have isolated a configuration of "myths" about women and work that continue to operate in people's minds and to effect discrimination against women in employment.

The publication of Betty Friedman's *The Feminine Mystique* in 1963 was a signal of the resurgence of American Feminism. Her sensitive and provocative analysis of the plight of the American woman rang true for thousands of women and sparked the flames of considerable feminist reflection and activity. The above publication points out that the highest value and the only commitment for women is the fulfilment of their own femininity. It says that the great mistake of Western culture through most of its history, has been the under-valuation of this femininity.

To conclude, women, all over the world, are enjoying a status of inferiority compared to that of male persons. However, philosophers as well as activists are trying to bring improvement in the position of women in all countries. The ancient proverbs and beliefs have changed to a great extent in favour of women of all countries. Both the liberal and radical feminists of the present believe that equality, justice and identity of women are the goals of today, if the society would be an advanced one with full participation of all its citizens.

REFERENCES

1. Nair, Jeevan, 1993-94, "The Second Sex", *Indian Journal of Public Administration*, p.11.
2. Pandey, Mrinal, 1994, "Gender, Poverty and Caste on a Pilgrimage", *Mainstream*, Vol. XXX, No.24, April 4.
3. Krishnaraj, Maithreyi, 1988, *Women and Development : The Indian Experience*, Shubhad Saraswat Prakashan. Pune, pp.20-22.
4. George, J. 1993, "Adjustment with Gender Equity", *Mainstream*, Vol. XXXI, No.20, March 27.
5. Heptulla, Najma, 1993, "Global Action Against Gender Discrimination, *Yojana*, Vol. 37, No.10, June 15.
6. Sahaya, Kumud, *Women in Focus, A Community in Search of Equal Roles*, 1984 Sangam Books (India) Pvt. Ltd. pp.73-86.
7. Quoted in R.K. Sapru, 1989, *Women and Development*, Ashish Publishing House, New Delhi, p.315.
8. Bhushan, L.I. and Rambha Prasad, 1993, *Concern for Status among Educated Women*, Classical Publishing Co., New Delhi, p.1.
9. Pujari, Premlata, and Vijay Kumari Kaushik, 1994, *Women Power in India : Institutional Systems for Women's Development*, Kaniska Publishers & Distributors, Delhi.
10. Pandey, Sumana, 1990, *Women in Politics*, Rawat Publications, Jaipur, pp.100-107.
11. Mehta, Rama, *Socio-Legal Status of Women in India*, Mittal Publications, Delhi, pp.11-12.

12. Charvet, John, 1982, *Modern Ideological Feminism*, J.M. Dent & Sons, Ltd., London, Melbourne and Toronto, pp.1-2.
13. Shah, Kalpana, "Modern Feminism : A Way to Liberation or Subjugation" in *Women's Liberation and Voluntary Action*, Ajanta Publications, New Delhi, pp.134-145.
14. Ahuja, Ram, 1992, *The Rights of Women : A Feminist Perspective*, Rawat Publications, Jaipur.

2

MANU MISUNDERSTOOD: A FRESH LOOK AT HIS ATTITUDE TOWARDS WOMEN

Dr. Harihar Mishra

Manu, the first law-giver of India has been strongly criticised by many of the feminists of today as against the liberation of women. Even the radical feminists went to the extent of an attempt to burn *Manusmruti* the great contribution of Manu to the Indian society and civilisation. Manu has been consistently charged with the criticism that he was against any kind of freedom or independence of women and he is thus, responsible for the age-old traditional inferior role and subjugation of women in Indian society. But Manu and his great work *Manusmruti* are not properly understood by the feminists, social activists, policy-makers as well as by the scholars for which, Manu's ideas about the role and status of women in society are misrepresented. Since, it is not possible to deal with all the so called controversial areas of the *Dharmasashtra*, the present paper discusses only one aspect of the work, that is, status of women in Aryan social order.

Manu has been criticised as the champion of the concept that women should enjoy an inferior status in the family, which forms the nucleus of all social systems. In this context, the critics take into account some portions of a statement of Manu, which occur in Chapter IX of the *Manusmruti*. This portion has been translated from Sanskrit to English as "Women are not fit for independence or liberty. All their activities should be kept under strict surveillance from cradle to burial ground."[1]

Here the translation appears to be wrong and when somebody quotes this portion alone, the original statement of Manu seems to lose its contextual relevance. For a clear understanding of Manu's attitude towards women, one should go through the whole text or at least through two chapters, namely, Chapter III and Chapter IX. These two chapters show the individual (irrespective of sex) the way to lead a perfect life after liberation from the attraction of *Artha* and *Kama* and move towards *Mokshya.*[2]

The English translation of the most controversial *sloka* of Manu is that a women never enjoys freedom in her life. "Her father protests her in childhood, her husband protect her in your, and her son protects her in her old age; a woman is never fit for independence."[3] Here the Sanskrit word *Swatantrya* has been translated as independence. But, in the context of the whole statement the translation seems to be wrong. Though Motwani uses a moderate word for it as "unguarded",[4] it is also equally unacceptable. That is why, great orientalists like Late P.V. Kane[5], Bhagwan Das[6], and K.P. Jaiswal[7] have not made any translation of this word into English. From its use in the writings of these scholars, it appears that "Swatantrya" is a typical Sanskrit word without any appropriate English rendering.

On the other hand, if one goes through the oldest explanation of the *Smruti Sastra* of Modhatithi[8], he will be doubly sure that the actual theme of the *Sloka* is that at no stage of life a woman should be thrown uncared for. She is to be cared of all stages of her life, because, creation "starts with her".[9] Therefore, Manu in this *Sloka* does not think woman unfit for independence; rather, he is of the opinion that women occupy a special status in the social whole simply by virtue of their being women and they should not go uncared for or feel like going so at any stage of their life.

Had it not been the intention of Manu to give women a special status in social order, he would not have give them highest status in his *Sastra*.[10] As Nitya Narayan Banerjee puts it,

> "Manu has not accepted the principle of equal status in the society for a man and woman. Each group has been assigned proper place of respect in his own respective sphere. Women have been given the highest status in the household. The husband has been ordained to keep his wife in good humour...Because, where women are not honoured, Gods forsake those households, says Manu (Ch. III, Sl. 55-62; Ch. IX, Sl. 26). Mother has been placed at much higher a position than that of the father, (Ch. II, Sl.145)."[11]

But as a psychologist, Manu did not hesitate to point out the eternal frailties and weaknesses of woman's mind and prescribe panacea for it. He has considered chastity and not beauty as the highest virtue of a woman. Purity of family blood and family heritage can only be maintained in the best interest of the society by preserving the chastity of woman. A good society, after all, can only be built with good families. Hence, Manu does not allow personal freedom for women to indulge in sensual or sexual pleasure in the best interest of the society as a whole.

It is the speciality with Manu (among ancient writers or *Shastrakaras*) that he "expressly regards the family as the unit of society."[12] Father-Mother-Child, those three together make up a complete man and a family.[13] Bhagvan Das[14] has rightly pointed out that modern tendency is to regard the individual as such unit. Individualism at one end and nationalism at the other end is the modern ideal. Familism at one end and humanism at the other is the ancient ideal. When the family is regarded as the unit, and the father, mother and child are regarded as permanently bound together, the natural consequence of paternal and maternal relationships stretching endlessly is that the whole society is seen to be of only psychologically but also biologically bound together and made cooperative. To be very specific, family is the individual writ large and the society is the family writ large. Therefore, Manu has prescribed stringent rules for governing the character of every unit of family for a perfect society, which is nothing other than the combination of perfect families and women are no exception to it. Since they play the most vital role in the family they need some extra care and protection. Therefore, Manu wrote that father protects women during childhood, in youth, they need protection from their husband and sons protect them during their old age. Women, therefore, should not be left unprotected.

In fact, this statement of Manu is mistaken to mean that the several male relations of the women are to sit tight over their rights and deny any freedom to them. This interpretation is against the spirit of Manu and imports extraneous considerations. What Manu states is that the marriage of the husband and wife implies such a complete merger of the two partners that their separate identity is lost and in the eye of law, they become a single juristic person. The juristic personality of the daughter vests in the father, of wife in her husband, and of the widow in her sons. Therefore, the woman is not to be treated as an independent juristic person. The legal implication of this principle is to confer absolute immunity on the woman from being made auctionable and dragged before a court of law. No claim against a daughter, a wife or a widow can be entertained by any competent authority because the woman has no jurisdiction of her own. It was never said by Manu that a woman could not own property. As a matter of fact, he has mentioned several sources by which property can accrue on a woman. For example, Manu mentions six kinds of *Stridhana.*[15] This interpretation of the statement of Manu is in perfect agreement with his other dictum in which he says that the 'person' of the husband and the wife are co-extensive and identical. "As a matter of fact, Manu's statements for and against women, as embodied in the Ninth Chapter represent two sides of a controversy and the verses relating to encomium bestowed on women form the *Uttarpakshya.* Of his argument.[16]

A careful, critical and scientific study of the *Manusmruti* shows that Manu is staunch believer i coordinated and harmonious development of human personality. He assigns a very reasonable place to women in the framework of society. He downs not regard them as necessary evils to be tolerated anyhow but, as the prime factor in man's worldly as well as spiritual happiness[17]. Man can not make any progress, if there be no women standing by his side ready to cooperate with him in all his activities. Man's power lies dormant so long as he is not touched he spark of woman's love and affection. The wheel of the world can not move in the absence of women.[18]

To conclude, critics have done little justice to this ancient lawgiver by misrepresenting him through a wrong interpretation of his ideas as contained in English translations of the original work. But before criticising somebody, we must take into account the time and the prevailing social system that was in operation when the *Sastra* was written.[19] That is the primary duty of the historians to find out the prevailing social system and culture of the time. Prof. Romila Thaper opines:

"It is a strange paradox that the historian who is concerned professionally with the past, plays a crucial role in the future of the society, which he is studying. The historian's interest lies in trying to understand the emergence and the evolution of a society in a historical perspective, where the term `society' includes every aspect of a people's life. As a result his investigations, the historian creates a picture of the society. In his landing of the evidence from the past, he is often influenced by his own contemporary setting. Historical interpretation, can therefore become a two-way process, where the needs of the present read into the past, the where the image of the past is ought to be imposed on the present. The image of the past is the historian's contribution to the future."[20]

REFERENCES

1. Mehta, Hans, 1981, women in Ancient India, New Delhi, Butala and Co., pp. 95-99. See also, W.M. Theodore De Berry and others (eds.), 1988, Introduction to Oriental Civilisation: Sources of Indian Tradition, New Delhi, Motilal Banarasidass, p.232.
2. For details, see Das, Bhagwan, 1948, The Science of Social Organisation or The Laws of Manu in the Light of Atmavidya, Vol. III, 2nd Edition, Banaras, Ananda Publishing House, pp. 763-869.
3. Buhler, John 1988, *The Sacred Books of the East Series,* Vol. XXV, New Delhi, Motilal Banarasidass, p. 328.
4. Motwani, Kewal, 1958, *Manu Dharmasastra,* New Delhi, Motilal Banarasidass, p. 100.
5. See Kane, P.V., 1974, *History of Dharmasastra,* Vol. II, Part-1, Poona, Bhandarakar Oriental Research Institute, pp. 340-347.
6. Das, Bhagwan, 1948, *op. cit.*
7. Jayaswal, K.P., 1978, *Hindu Polity,* Bangalore, The bangalore Printing and Publishing Company. See also, Prabhu, P.H., 1991, *Hindu Social Organisation: A Study in Socio-Psychological and Ideological Foundations,* Bombay, Popular Prakashan, pp. 201-256.
8. Medhatithi is accepted as the first authoritative interpreter of the *Manusmruti* published by the Gurumandal Granthamela, Calcutta in 1916.
9. Sastri, R. Shama, 1977, *Evolution of Indian Polity,* Delhi Nag Publishers, First Reprint, pp. 1-4.
10. See *Manusmruti,* Chapters II and III.
11. Banerjee, Nitya Narayan, 1975, *Manu and Modern Times,* New Delhi, Hindutva Publications, pp. 9-10.
12. Das Bhagwan, *op. cit.,* p.776.
13. See *Manusmruti,* Chapter IV, Sloka 45.
14. Das Bhagwan, *op. cit.,* p. 776.

15. See *Manusmruti*, Chapter IV, Sloka 194.
16. Agarwala, V.S., 1962. "Introduction", in R.M. Das, *Women in Manu and His Seven Commentators*, Bodh Gaya, Kanitan Publications, p. XV.
17. . Das, R.N., 1962, *op. cit.*, p. 38.
18. *Manusmruti*, Chapter IV, Sloka 27 and 28.
19. See Altekar, A.S., 1983, *The Position of Women in Hindu Civilisation*, Delhi, Motilal Banarasidass, pp. 234-235.
20. Thapar, Romila, 1975, The Past and Prejudice, New Delhi, National Book Trust, p.1.

3

WOMEN IN INDIA: PAST AND PRESENT

Dr. (Mrs.) Navaneeta Rath

The human society is everywhere composed of males and females and the society is stratified on the basis of sex. Women constitute half of the population and thus, a significant segment of every society. Hence, their status, role and position determine the progress and development of the society as well as identify the culture and values on which the society is based.

India has a long past civilization and in every stage of its history, women constitute half of its population, but their position in society is not the same in all the ages of history. Their position has been variously estimated and diametrically opposite views are current regarding their place in different stages of Indian civilisation.[1] Several factors including foreign invasions for centuries together, social movements, various geographic regions, different economic occupations, political stability and instability and religious affinity of the family to which woman belongs have always greatly influenced her status in the family as well as in the community.[2]

However, for the sake of analysis, the position of women in India can be studied in different phases of history, namely, in Ancient India, in British India, and in post-independent India.

WOMEN IN ANCIENT INDIA

More than two thousand years ago, the *Rigveda*, the *Upanishad*, Kautilya's *Arthasastra* and many other writings reveal that women in India enjoyed a fair measure of equality with men in all spheres of human activity – spiritual and religious, teaching and learning, even war and statecraft. The *Rig Veda* propagated that reality consists of two aspects, that is, male and female. Except Hindu religious scriptures, no where it is written that male and female are counterparts of each other, both are complimentary to each other, and both in the form of *Shiva* and *Sakti* constitute the *Nature*. Hindu religion provides the concept of unity of male and female, which equally contribute for sustaining the Reality. Further, the woman in traditional religious belief has been regarded as the Universal Mother. The common metaphor used to describe her as *Prithivi* (Mother earth), who upholds all the living and non-living beings. Finally, she had been portrayed as *Prakriti*, while male had been described as *Purusa*. Hence, *Prakriti* and *Purusa*, female and male together constitute the Reality or Nature. This religious dictate determined the equal virtue of women in family and in society. During the Vedic period, education was imparted to both male and female child. In fact, the education of women was looked upon as so important that the *Atharva Veda* asserts that "the success of woman in her married life depends upon her proper training during the Brahmacharya." Hence, the girls like the boys had to undergo the initiation, the *Samskar*, *Upanayan* and *Brahmacharya*. They were also allowed to perform *Sandhya* rites like the male persons. Women thus, learnt and recited *Vedas* and took part in conferences and deliberations and in this context, the names of women like Lopamudra, Brahmavadini, Gargi etc. are still heard as the most learned philosopher women of Vedic age.

Even when, Buddhism and Jainism were spread in ancient India, both these religions did not make any gender discrimination, so far as education and religious preaching were concerned. The women during this period undertook equal pain like male missionaries by travelling far and wide for preaching the messages of Lord Buddha. They led a life of celibacy and became prophets of Holy Scriptures. The Buddhist history still carries the messages of the famous nun Ambapalli and the missionary Sanghamitra, daughter of King Ashok who even reached Ceylon to spread Buddhist teachings. Similar was the case of Jainism, as one of the Great 24 Tirthankars of Jainism was Mali, daughter of King Videha.

Not only did the women of ancient India were imparted with religious education, but they were also well equipped with military and administrative training. Of course, the women of ruling elite class families were given this type of training. To give illustration, we may cite from history Dowager Queens, Nayanika of Satavahana dynasty (2nd century B.C.), Prabhavati Gupta of Vakataka family (4th century A.D.), Vijayabhattarika of Chalukya House (7th century A.D.), and Sugandha and Didda of Kashmir (10th century A.D.), who successfully administered extensive kingdoms.[3]

The social status of women during this period was also very illuminating. Girls had their effective say in choosing their life partners and also in the marriage affair. *Swayamvara* was an accepted practice among the Kshetriyas in ancient India. Girls, after obtaining puberty became eligible to marry. Child-marriage was rare. So, before marriage, women were well-equipped with education and training. Even, pre-marital and extra-marital affairs of the women were not looked down by the social norms of ancient India. As Prof. Mazumdar observes, "Even wives suspected of paramours were not denied social and religious rites, far less driven away from the family."[4] Prostitution, though existed as a rare phenomenon, did not degrade the status of women in the society of the ancient period. The Rig Veda, the Buddhist *Jataka* mention that prostitution was treated as a part of the social system and was not totally absent in the society. Nevertheless, the prostitutes also commanded a certain amount of status in the society and they were economically well paid. The other manifestation of prostitution was found in the accepted custom of dancers in the king's palaces and *Devdasis* in the Hindu temples. Elopement, though unusual, was not negatively sanctioned.[5]

Further, in ancient India, there was the provision for widow marriage. According to *Narada Smriti*, widows could remarry, if their husbands died or they were impotent. Property would be granted, if the widow married a person approved by her father-in-law.[6] Levitate (the custom by which a dead man's brother or next of kin married the widow) was sanctioned and was extensively practised in ancient India. Subbamma[7] suggests that *Sati* was not approved though, there was a mention of it in the *Atharva Veda*. But, S.K. Ghosh argues that the archaic system of *Sati* prevailed at the beginning of the Vedic age.[8] It was however, discontinued when the Aryans found it necessary to encourage the widows to live and increase the population by Niyoga and remarriage. There were stray cases of *Sati* in the *Mahabharat*. For example, Madri committed *Sati* on the funeral pyre of her husband, Pandu. But the *Ramayan* bears no case of *Sati*.

Worship of Goddess was a common practice in ancient Indian society. Archaeological excavations, historical documents provide ample illustrations of the worship of female deities in the country, which is a reflection of the high and exalted social status of women in the society. Hence, Dr. Radhakrishnan rightly observes, "Indian tradition has generally respected womanhood, though occasionally we find derogatory references to women."[9]

However, the status of women became lowered down from about 300 B.C., when the Aryans encountered various tribal people, who inhabited the Gangetic Plains. The Aryans took recourse to invasion and needed male child to fight in the battle-field. The expectation for a male child gradually reduced the status of a woman. Furthermore, because of the availability of the cheap manual labour of the vanquished non-Aryans, the need for women labour in agriculture and in production of goods was reduced. At this point, Altekar observes, "the women became less productive members of the society and that indirectly lowered their status."[10]

The uneducated non-Aryan women outnumbered the educated Aryan women and this number had got a negative force for maintaining the equal and respectable status and identity of women in society. Gradually, all women, Aryan and Non-Aryan, became ineligible to study *Veda* as well as for ritual duties. This position of women was supported by *Manu Samvita,* the first law-code for Hindus in India which provided a dependent and thus subservient status to women in India. Manu had made a sex-based division of society and offered a lower position to women in the social ladder of the hierarchical organization of the society. To Manu, a girl has to depend on her father during childhood, on her husband during her youth, and on her son when she became old. A woman cannot do anything even in her own house by being a young girl, a young woman or even by being an aged woman. So Manu set a series of chains for the woman where from liberation became difficult and the secondary position of women became the traditional order of society since those days.

The deprivation of women from Vedic studies and ritual duties was accompanied by the vicious social customs like early marriage, *Sati,* and widowhood which made the position of women in society very worse. Child marriage which started from around 500 B.C. and continued for a long time as a social custom had made women silent in choosing their life-partners. Women, losing their own identity and freedom became individuals to be treated with pity and sympathy in their in-laws' house. Marriage was treated more as an alliance between two families than a union of two souls with equal and reciprocal love and affection. In this connection, it becomes worth-quoting the ideas of thinkers like, Meheta[11], Kapadia[12], and Rose[13], who subscribe the view that "marriage in Hindu orthodoxy was not a selection between two families", "a social duty towards the family and community". Joint family system, which became an established social institution during this period, had its adverse effect, so far as the status of women was concerned. Dubois, in making an analysis of Hindu customs and ceremonies made a keen observation that the concentration of authority in the head of the family left an unhealthy influence for younger members who lived in a state of subordination, which obscured personal liberty and prevented development of inner talent. This is specially marked in the case of women.[14]

Again, during this period, ban on widow remarriage lowered down the position of women in society. Widowhood became a curse and was considered as a result of sin committed by the women. A widow had to lead a very torturous, miserable and unbearable life-style, till she went to the graveyard. She was physically exploited, mentally tortured, and economically deprived of the property of her deceased husband. Being deprived also of participating in socio-religious ceremonies of the family and the community, she was a hatred fellow for whom life was a curse. As a result, woman preferred to immolate themselves on the funeral pyre of their husbands, which created another evil institution, *Sati,* in Indian society. When women were forced to immolate themselves against their own volition, it became an inhuman and brutal treatment towards women. If the women became barren, then they were treated as inauspicious persons in society.

This state of affairs of women became more deteriorated with the constant invasion of our land by enemies like Moghuls and Marathas. Social institutions broke down and society suffered a cultural collapse in India. Women became a prey in the hands of the invaders to be tortured, both physical and mental. In order to protect the women from cruel hands of the invaders, they were to be hidden inside the house and the safest place for them became hearth and home. This led to a number of evil practices, like ban on women's education, widow-marriage and exposure of women outside the home etc., which gave rise to the customs like child marriage, polygamy, *purdah* system and deprivation of women from property ownership etc. Hence, in medieval India, the woman's status both socially and economically was reduced to one of inferiority, backward, secondary, and unequal.

WOMEN IN PRE-INDEPENDENCE PERIOD

The reformist wind blew in the direction of emancipation of women for the first time in India during the 19th century. The great thinkers in this direction were Raja Rammohun Roy, Ishwar Chandra Vidyasagar, Dayanand Saraswati, Swami Vivekanand and Mahatma Gandhi. The ideas of the social reformers became manifested to some extent by the laws enacted by the British Government in India. In 1829, the first social law was enacted by Lord William Bentinck to abolish *Sati* and to declare it a crime. Simultaneously, the Brahmo Samaj established by Raja Rammohun Roy stood for the principle of freedom of women and equality of sexes. He vehemently opposed *Sati* and campaigned for widow marriage. All these ideologies were reflected through the publications particularly, in *Sambad Kaumudi* published by him. Ishwar Chandra Vidyasagar took leading part in promulgating the Widow Remarriage Act of 1856 to make the widow marriage legal as well as to provide a status to Hindu widow in society. In order to prevent child widowhood, another great landmark of the 19th century was the Civil Marriage Act of 1872, which raised the age for marriage of the girls to fourteen and enforced monogamy.

During the National Struggle for Independence, Gandhiji gave a clarion call for emancipation of women from household drudgery and to join the movement for the freedom of the country. He was very well aware of the fact that if fifty per cent of the population being women would not join the movement and remain alienated from it, the non-violent struggle based upon people's participation would not be successful. Hence, it was Gandhiji's bidding that, women in large numbers came out from their homes and stood shoulder to shoulder with men in the struggle for freedom and this became unprecedented in Indian history. Gandhiji gave even a superior status to women. So he wrote, "I am uncompromising in the matter of women's rights. The difference in sex and physical form denotes no difference in status. Woman is the complement of man, and not inferior." Further, he says, "To call woman the weaker sex is libel. It is man's injustice to woman. If by strength is meant brute strength, then indeed, woman is less brute than man. If by strength is meant moral power, then woman is immeasurably man's superior." Further, he wrote, "Woman is the companion of man gifted with equal mental capacities. She has the right to participate in the minutest details of the activities of man, and she has the same right of freedom and liberty as he...by sheer force of a vicious custom, even the most important and worthless men have been enjoying a superiority over women which they do not deserve and ought not to have."[15] Swami Vivekananda also gave a very high status to women in India, when he said, "That country and that nation which did not respect women have never become great nor will ever in the future."

Being inspired by the social reformers and national leaders, a large number of women came out and joined the freedom struggle. They formed a number of women's organizations to create social and political consciousness among the women for their rights, equality and uplift as well as for their participation in the freedom struggle. The first women's organization was the Indian Women's Association, which started working in 1917 by Mrs. Margaret Cousins under the leadership of Mrs. Annie Besant and her Home Rule Movement. Mrs. Annie Besant was elected as the President of the Calcutta Session of Indian National Congress, and for the first time, in this session, the opinion was expressed that "the same tests be applied to women as to men in regard to franchise and the eligibility of all elective bodies concerned with the local government and education." Thus, the Indian National Congress recognized officially the equality of sexes in politics. In 1927, Smt. Kamla Devi Chattopadhyaya organized the All India Women's Conference and adorned the chair of its General Secretary. Similarly, Sarojini Naidu's contribution to the renaissance of Indian womanhood cannot be underestimated. It was her call for the women's section of the Congress that led to the formation of the All India Women's Conference. Similar roles were played by Raj Kumari Amrit Kaur, Mridula Sarabai, Sucheta Kripalini, Padmja Naidu, Durgabai Deshmukh, Aruna Asaf Ali and many other great women of India who set golden foot-prints for the arise, awake, and emancipation of women for their freedom, equality and identity as well as for their contribution to the nation' freedom.

WOMEN IN POST-INDEPENDENCE PERIOD

The first task in post-independent India was to provide a Constitution to the people of India and the spirit behind the Constitution was to bridge every gap between the citizens of India, so far as right, equality and development were concerned. Hence, the Constitution does not make any distinction on the basis of sex and provides rights, freedom, and privileges equally to both men and women. The Preamble of the Constitution promises to secure to all its citizens,

> JUSTICE, social, economic and political;
> LIBERTY of thought, expression, belief; Faith and worship;
> EQUALITY of status and of opportunity and to promote among them all

FRATERNITY assuring the dignity of the individual and the unity and integrity of the Nation

Further, the Constitution declares that the equality before the law and the equal protection of laws shall not be denied to any person on the ground of sex. (Art.14). Similarly, there shall be no discrimination against any citizen on the ground of sex. (Art, 15). Art.15 (1) guarantees "equality of opportunity" for all citizens in matters relating to employment or appointment to any office under the state and forbids discrimination in respect of any employment of office under the state on the grounds of sex. Art.19 provides certain fundamental rights, such as, freedom of speech and expression, to assemble, to form associations, to move freely, to reside and settle in any part of the country and to practice any profession to both men and women of India equally. Art.25 also provides right to freedom to both men and women. Art. 326 provides universal adult franchise, that is, equal participation of men and women in politics.

Apart from the equality to women along with the men guaranteed by the Constitution, the Constitution also makes certain provisions for special privileges for women. Art.15(3) proclaims that the State can make any special provision for women and children. Nevertheless, Directive Principles of State Policy which concern women directly and have a special bearing on their status include Art.39(a) right to an adequate means of livelihood; (d) equal pay for equal work both for men and women; (e) protection of health and strength of workers – men, women and children and Art.42 provides for just and humane conditions of work and maternity relief.

Amongst the Personal Laws made for raising the status of women is the Uniform Civil Code which was enacted by Parliament in 1955-56. It is the first step in evolving a uniform Civil Code for the entire Indian people and in removing disabilities of law. It reformed the Hindu Law relating to (i) marriage and divorce, (ii) succession, and (iii) adoption, and

(iv) minority and guardianship. The Anti-dowry Act of 1961 prohibits dowry system and thereby makes the woman equal partner with man so far as property is concerned. The daughter, the widow and the mother now inherit property along with the son. Several laws against dowry, rape and immoral traffic have been enacted.[16]

During the U.N. Decade for Women, the Government of India constituted a Committee on the Status of Women by a resolution of the Ministry of Education and Social Welfare on 22nd September 1971. The Committee was entrusted with the task of making a comprehensive examination of all questions relating to the rights and status of women in India and to provide useful guidelines for the formulation of social policies. Accordingly, the Committee examined the present position of women in India and recommended for raising the social, legal and economic status of women in order to bring about equality of sexes. The Committee laid emphasis on emancipation and freedom of women through employment and income generation programmes. Empowerment of women through education and employment formed the core of the suggestions laid down by the Committee.

Though the Constitution of India is working since more than forty-five years and social laws are enacted, the raising of the status of women to one of equality, freedom and dignity is still a question mark. The very fact that the numerical strength of women is declining during these years raises doubt relating to the improved status of women. The table given below exhibits the picture of declining trend of the numerical strength of women in India.

Except 1981, in the entire census decades the number of women is declining. Several reasons may be attributed for this trend, such as, (a) carelessness of parents for a girl baby during her birth and during her infancy, (b) unwillingness of parents to provide medical and other facilities for the survival of girl child and finally, (c) the misuse of amniocentesis to kill a female fetus. Of course, the Government of India now has enacted the law against the misuse of amniocentesis.

TABLE – 1

Sex Ratio in India as per 1, 000 Males

Year	*Female Sex Ratio*
1951	946
1961	941
1971	930
1981	934
1991	927

Source: Census of India Publications

Education is one of the important indices of the socio-economic status of the individual in society. Education is not only insurance for the women at the time of odd, but also an assurance for the full-fledged development of her personality, and through that for the society. It will enlighten her instead of confusing her. The correlation between several development indicators and the level of female literacy can not be underestimated as education is positively related with women's participation in modern economy, in development, in environment protection and in political process. Realizing the importance of women's education, the University Education Commission, 1948-49 stated that "There can not be educated people without educated women. If general education had to be limited to men or to women, that opportunity should be given to women, for then, it would most surely be passed on to the next generation."

The Constitution of India guarantees equal opportunities for education without any gender bias and it directs the state to endeavor to provide for free and compulsory education for all children until they complete the age of fourteen years. But, what is the state of affair with female education? It is true that cent per cent literacy is still a dream for the people of India. Nevertheless, the gender discrimination in the field of education is very unfortunate and sordid affair. The following table gives the picture of female literacy.

TABLE – 2

Literacy Rate of Males and Females in India

Census Year	*Male Literacy (%)*	*Female Literacy (%)*
1951	27.16	8.86
1961	40.40	15.54
1971	45.95	21.97
1981	56.37	29.78
1991	63.86	39.42

Of course, the literacy rate of females is increasing through these years, but the rate of progress is very slow and disheartening. In comparison to male literacy there are less female literate persons and if the higher education will be taken into account, the number of females will be very marginal. It is more disheartening when we take the picture of 1991 Census Report that while more than two-thirds of women live in rural areas, female literacy rate is 25.13% as against 54.01% in urban areas.

This fact became more vivid when the Committee on the Status of Women (1975) asserted that "the image of the Indian women created by a few women holding high positions or academic qualifications conceals rather than reflecting the status and education level of the average woman of India." In opening the discussion on "Education for Women's Equality", The National Policy on Education (1986), points out that "Provision of educational opportunities to women has been an important programme in the education sector since independence", but observes that "inspite of the efforts made so far, the education system has not been able to make sufficient contribution towards women's equality." In the same vein, the *National Perspective Plan for Women, 1988-2000* notes that "Education of women occupies top priority among various measures taken to improve the status of women in India" and that "great emphasis has been laid on women's education in the Five Year Plans". But, the same Report points out that "notwithstanding the planned objectives and endeavours, actual progress in upgrading the educational status of women has been slow."

The reasons for keeping the girls away from getting education are namely, (1) poverty, (2) conservative social and cultural values and beliefs, (3) gender discrimination, and (4) lack of infra-structural facilities.

Combined with the low educational profile of women, the health neglect is very much prominent which exhibits the lower status of women in India even today. Gender bias in rearing up the female child is still happening to be a lingering paradox. The average expectation of life at birth for females though is in a process of constant increase, yet it has not come in par with that of males. Infant mortality of females is more than that of the males due to the general health neglect of a female child by the parents. There still remains a gap between the life expectancy of a male and that of a female. The women are more undernourished than the male persons are and V.Rajalakshmi rightly observes, "quite often he root cause of malnutrition among girls is not so much lack of food as the lack of access to food. Undernourished girls who grow into undernourished women perpetuate the inter-generations undernourishment cycle."[17] In fact, ICMR data of 1955 and NNMB data of 1975 demonstrate that there is "no evidence of secular trends indicating improved growth performance in the succeeding generation – a feature expected of all successful developing societies."[18] Women in India thus take insufficient dietary intake of calories, proteins, calcium, iron, and vitamin A. As per estimation, two-thirds of Indian pregnant women are anaemic. They do not take accurate nutritious food intake, nor they accept the health facilities provided for them. Mrs. Gopalan of Nutritious

Foundation of India in her Report (1987) on caloric intake and nutrition assessment reveals that poor nutrition standard is a constant headache of health and morbidity status of girl child in India, which needs special care and action-oriented programmes. The mass immunisation and regular health check-up of school children are necessary.

Work participation of women in post-independent India is also not encouraging. Women labour hard in household management and also outside, they get less wages and in terms of cash money her labour is not properly paid. During these years, the Indian economy has witnessed a structural transformation particularly in favour of industrial sector and service sector. In these two sectors, work participation of women is very marginal. This is due to the fact that women lack proper education, training and skill to hold jobs in these two sectors of economy and moreover, the dynamics of gender differentiation – female inefficacy and female subordination have been transmitted outside the home over to these two sectors of the economy. Women are found in greater number in labour market, which is considered as secondary work characterised by low status of employment, less wages, occupational immobility, particularly of employment, less use of skill and training etc. As per 1981 Census Report, the female work participation is only 14 per cent while that of male is 51.6%. When we make the rural-urban divide, it is found as per the above Census Report that in urban area, the female work participation rate is only 10.7%, while that of rural area is 23.9%. "Though majority of women in comparable age-groups of men are engaged in work, but since many works performed by women within the household sector do not have pecuniary value, they have been excluded from worker status, and the bias is more pronounced in urban India."[19] The table given below indicates the work-force participation of both males and females.

However, it is found that in 1981, more than 80 per cent

TABLE – 3

Work-force Participation Rate in India by Sex, Rural and Urban Areas, 1981.

(in percentage)

Category	*Total*	*Male*	*Female*	*Rural*	*Male*	*Female*	*Urban*	*Male*	*Female*
Main Workers	33.5	51.62	13.99	34.76	52.62	16.0	29.23	48.54	7.28
Marginal Workers	3.32	1.03	5.77	4.11	1.19	7.18	0.77	0.53	1.04
Total Workers	36.77	52.65	19.76	38.87	53.81	23.18	30.00	49.07	8.32

Source: Report of the Census of India, 1981.

of women were engaged in the primary sector occupations thereby clearly establishing the marginal occupational status of Indian women even after more than thirty years of independence. This became more vivid when compared to the male employed persons. Women are underrepresented in many important occupations like professional and related work; administrative, executive, and managerial work as well as in the fields of science and technology. Even, as Rehman and Biswal[20] have pointed out that the status of women in labour market is marginal. Their contribution to production activities still goes unrecognised. The perception about their nature of work has not yet been economically termed. Though they work harder than their male counterparts and the total hours of a day their work is more than that of men, so far, no effort has been made to develop such indicators which would measure their share in the processes of production, distribution and consumption. The irony is that, they are not earning cash money, wages or salary. In other words, they have been discriminated against both outside and within the labour market in India. Within the labour market, they are discriminated against at the point of entry into well paid and high status occupations, though no one has yet proved the so-called proposition of less productivity of women in some jobs in which they are underrepresented.

So far as the social position of women in India today is concerned, two opposite views have come to the forefront. One view is that women have now become free from the evil chains of traditional joint family system. In the nuclear family system, the wife finds herself next to her husband in taking decisions in household affairs and in shaping the domestic economy. Similarly, the marriage system has undergone a lot of change. Due to the enactment of social laws, spread of female education and due to the growth of professionalism in every sphere, the marriage age of the male and female has gone up and child marriage has become a rare phenomenon. Marriage is no more, an obligatory fact on the part of the women. "The modern women of the country today does not view marriage as a sole necessity but one among many aspects of home, marital comforts, good health and youthfulness."[21]

But marriage system in its changed form has brought with it the ugly practice of dowry, which has resulted in degradation of he status of women in the post-independent India. Neera K. Sohoni [22] describes that dowry as a marital custom obviously enhances the status of the boy and devalues that of the girl with similar impact on the status of their respective families. Dowry has come to be demanded as a matter of right by the bridegroom and his family. If not forthcoming, there is a pressure applied to extract or even to extort it. Her future becomes threatened by the possibility of the marriage breaking up. Worse still she is in the immediate danger of physical maltreatment and being alone in a strange household with no one on her side, she often actually suffers physical abuse. In any case, being constantly among hostile people, she loses her mental and psychological peace. [23] Ultimately, the women are to be killed or they sacrifice their life by suicide due to the non-fulfilment of dowry demanded by the bridegroom and his family. Hence, due to this ugly practice, the women have been treated as animate property and they are considered as puppets to dance in the tune of the male persons in her own family and in the family of the in-laws. She has got no independent voice to be raised either as a maiden or as a married woman. Obviously, she develops a fear psychosis of being a female and the parents due to the evil customs of the society make discrimination between a son and a daughter. As it is said earlier, longing for a male child reduces to a great extent the status of a female in the society.

Crime against women in present India has become alarming. Violence against women is rooted in the tradition of discrimination that has been going on for centuries. Dr. L.N. Mittal[24] writes, "Violence and crime against women in India are increasing every year whether at home, at the workplace, on the street, in custody or elsewhere. The recent report of Amnesty International on India has observed that women are regularly raped in jail cells in India.... A U.N. Report has also pointed out that India has the highest number of custodial rapes by men in positions of power. The recently brought out Data Sheet on "Violence against Women" by the Department of Women and Child Development, Ministry of Human Resource Development, Government of India, reveals that a woman is raped somewhere in India every 54 minutes, a molestation takes place in every 26 minutes, one kidnapping or abduction every 43 minutes. One act of eve-teasing every 51 minutes, one dowry death every 102 minutes and one act of criminal offence against women committed every seven minutes. Taking the statistics of only one year 1991, it is found that in India, there are 9793 rape cases, 20611 molestation cases, 5137 dowry death cases and 10283 eve teasing cases.

To conclude, the status of women in India has not been raised so much to be equal with the male persons. Women, though are entitled to equal constitutional and legal rights, do not enjoy them because of their ignorance, age long superstition, inferiority complex, and discrimination in a male-dominated society. Of course, in politics, in social organisation and movements, in economy and in development, the presence of women is remarkable, but their number is very less in proportion to the total number of women-folk and in proportion to male representation. Women are still considered as "weaker sex". They are regarded as only consumers, because, they are not economically independent. Women are still voiceless, as their participation in decision-making bodies is very marginal, and they still find themselves weak in taking decisions at home and outside independently. They are still considered more as wives and mothers than as citizens of India. There is a large gap between the enactment and enforcement of social laws for women. This can be bridged up only when women would be empowered through education to be conscious of their identity, dignity, and prestige.

Empowerment of women also depends upon the social esteem for multi-dimensional roles of women both inside and outside home. The dependence syndrome is to be totally changed to make women self-reliant, self-propelled and self-directed.

REFERENCES

1. Parmar, Y.S., 1973, *Polyandry in the Himalayas*, Vikas Publishing House Pvt. Ltd., p.33.
2. Gaur, Alkertine, 1980, *Women in India*, The British Library Series, London, p. 3.
3. Ghosh, S.K., 1989, *Indian Women through the Ages*, Ashis Publishing House, Delhi, p.5.
4. Majumdar, R.C., 1953, "Ideal and Position of Indian Women in Domestic Life", in Swami Madhavananda and R.C. Majumdar (eds.), Great Women of India, Almore, Advaita Ashram, p.10.
5. Mukherji, P.N., 1988, "Sex and Social Structure" in Karuna Channa, (ed.), Socialisation, *Education and Women: Explorations in Gender Identity*, Orient Longman, New Delhi, p.35.
6. Rodrigues, Clarissa, 1991, "Radhakrishnan's Views on Women: An Appraisal" in Sebasti L.Raj (ed.), *Quest for Gender Justice*, T.R. Publications, p.125.
7. Subbamma, M., 1987, *Women, Tradition and Culture*, Sterling Publications Pvt. Ltd., New Delhi, p.19.
8. Ghosh, S.K., *op.cit.*, p.8
9. Radhakrishnan, S., 1956, *Occasional Speeches and Writings*, October 1952 – January 1956, p.371.
10. Altekar, A.S., 1953, "Ideal and Position of Indian Women in Social Life" in *Great Women of India*, op. cit. P.30.
11. Mehta, R., 1970, *The Western Educated Hindu Women*, Asia Publishing House, Bombay, pp.17-18.
12. Kapadia, K.M., 1966, *Marriage and Family in India*, 3rd Edition, Oxford University Press, Calcutta, p.169.
13. Ross, E.D., 1973, *The Hindu Family in its Urban Setting*, Oxford University Press, Delhi, p.251.
14. Dubois, A.J.A., 1973, *Hindu Manners, Customs and Ceremonies*, translated by Henry K. Beauchamp, Indian Reprint, Mamata Publication, Delhi, pp.112 & 115.
15. Gandhi, M.K., 1918, *Young India*, February 26, pp.105-106.
16. The social laws were enacted during the British regime to create a social base for women to be equal with men. These laws are as follows:

(a) Prohibition of Sati System Act, 1829.
(b) Hindu Widow Remarriage Act, 1856.
(c) Indian Divorce Act, 1869.
(d) Special Marriage Act, 1872.
(e) Child Marriage Restraint Act, 1929.
(f) The Arya Marriage Validity Act, 1937.
(g) Hindu Widow's Right on Property Act, 1937.

17. Rajalakshmi, V. 1991, "Indian Women Today", in S.L. Raj, (ed.), *Quest for Gender Justice*, T.R. Publications, p.2.
18. Gopalan, C. and S. Kaur, (ed.), 1989, *Women and Nutrition in India*, NFI, New Delhi, p.2.
19. Rehman, M.M. and Kamalakanta Biswal, 1993, *Education, Work and Women, Commonwealth Publishers*, New Delhi, p.78.
20. Rehman and Biswal, 1993, *op.cit.*, p.92.
21. Kapur, Promila, 1974, *The Changing Status of Working Women in India*, Vikas Publishing House, New Delhi,
22. Sohoni, Neera K., 1994, *Status of Girls in Development Strategies*, New Delhi, p.31.
23. Atray, J.P., 1988, *Crimes Against Women*, Vikas Publishing House, New Delhi, p.73.
24. Mittal, L.K., 1993, "Crime Against Women", *Social Welfare*, Vol.XXXIX, No.11-12, Feb.-March, p.3.

4

WOMEN IN INDIAN SOCIETY: PROSPECTS AND PERCEPTIONS

Dr. R. Veeramani & T. Ravi

During the Vedic period, women seem to have enjoyed comparatively high status, despite male domination and the importance given to a 'Grahastha'. Over the centuries however, women's position evidently deteriorated and weakened. The right place of women was thought to be the house and the right work was only domestic chores. Several stringent rules were prescribed to them and that they were further subjugated. While women were glorified to the status of goddesses, their actual position was so miserable that they were treated mere chattels. Denied education or exposure to the outer world, women become ignorant partners, who seldom had a voice to fight for their position. The impossible virtues expected of women and the double standards of morality further lowered their position.

STATUS OF WOMEN IN INDIAN SOCIETY

In most society of the world, the documented evidence shows that women's primary role have been family oriented. It may be useful at this stage to review the status of women in Indian society. It is nevertheless, true that even in ancient times, there was a longing for the birth of a male child. But, the a female child was not to be killed, as it is happening today. In ancient times, women were given sufficient freedom to choose their partners and were allowed to remarry. They were, in general, assigned a high position in the society. But during the *Puranic* period, it was felt necessary to sublimate and glorify the unjust and traditional laws on women. One among them was the duty of married women. To attain eternal salvation, she was advised to do service to her husband and she was made to believe that it was the only primary duty in her life. *Puranas* were introduced to highlight this view in the most appealing form. It was during this period, some of the cruel practices like *Sati* came in practice in the Indian society. Welfare and dignity of the women were discouraged with religion and fanaticism. During the Moghul period, the enlightened Akbar sought to correct these cruel deformities of Hindu society through certain social reforms, but in vain.

The traditional norms of Indian society refused the free entry of women workers in the labour market. The women were also handicapped by the fact that, the level of literacy among them was low and there was no incentive and encouragement for their mass education. The strenuous boredom of their household work together with the high rate of pre-natal morbidity sapped the womenfolk of all their energy and enthusiasm in life, and thus, they were not in a position to clamor against the age-long suppression of their rights and privileges.

The advent of English education during the British Rule in India freed some of the men of the Indian society from the clutches of the traditional Hindu conservatism, and made them realise the inhuman treatment given to the Indian women. Raja Rammohun Roy was the pioneer social reformer in this direction. He vehemently protested against many of the cruel restrictions on women, and tried to review Hinduism in terms of its old *Vedic* glory through undermining the irrelevance of *Manusmruti*. The later acceptance of Raja Rammohun Roy's views gave rise to an era of social reforms of Hindu society even leading to extreme postures against the very concept of

Hinduism as done by Periyar E.V. Ramaswamy Naicker.

Social manifestations may be seen in the increasing incidences of dowry and the declining value of women due to the erosion of their economically and social productive roles. The process of development itself has undergone changes, which have widened and accentuated socio-economic inequalities.

Law, in general, does not rule women,, but they are ruled and controlled by customs and traditions. Legislation and its implementation by voluntary agencies is required on a very large scale to reach the mass of women and to enlighten them towards their rightful place in society.

One of the noteworthy features of the last four decades is the improved status of women in the country. Indian women have accomplished a great deal of improvement in their status in comparison to the status enjoyed by them previously. Indian women today, are also in a better position than those of many western countries, as they are entering in many white-collar jobs in large number. In India, women are also taking active part in politics. In matters like inheritance of property and separation from the house, women enjoy today greater freedom than before. It is quite true that the changes reported above are predominantly urban phenomena. In the rural areas also, changes in these directions are taking place, though slowly and imperceptibly. So, on the whole, it can be said that there has been substantial emancipation of our women from subjugation in a smooth and unaggressive manner.

EDUCATION AND WOMEN

Education has been considered as the crucial factor in movements for women's rights for equality, dignity or justice. Access of education for women determines their role in the economy and their freedom in most matters. Women's illiteracy is one of the most characteristic features of developing countries.

All over the world, including India, working class women work for the survival and maintenance of their families. The educational system itself sometimes, has become a very powerful instrument for maintaining class and sexual inequality in society. Mere expansion of educational opportunities for women or their increasing induction into different levels of the existing system, though an immediate necessity, will not in itself achieve equality or development, unless education itself undergoes qualitative, structural changes. Women's education has a critical role in national reconstruction.

The importance of women's education can be pronounced by quoting the words of Mahatma Gandhi: "You educate a man, you educate an individual, educate a woman, you educate a family." Therefore, it is assumed that education among women is all the more needed. The National Policy of Education (1986) has provided equal educational opportunities to women. The task is onerous. Such a goal can be attained with the participation of both the government and people.

WOMEN AND EMPLOYMENT

The social image of a woman today is that of an invader in man's world of employment. Further, being a competitor in the field of employment, she is an economic asset in the family. Woman is playing the ideal role by combining home-making and career. Woman's dual role is always between ambition and affection, and duty and devotion, if she considers the employment as essential one for her family.

There may be several reasons that motivate woman to venture into what is still essentially a man's world, leaving behind the security of home. Broadly the factors, which motivate women in going for employment, are three, namely, economic, boredom and desire for self-expression. However, the economic necessity ranks foremost importance among many reasons for the entry of women in formal sector. Women go for work to maintain a better standard of living, to pay off debt, to support dependents or relatives, to enable children to have better education or, because of rise in cost of living etc.

In India, now, many young girls are entering into salaried jobs, because, women employment is now in many cases, considered as a passport for marriage. In some cases, women use to work till their marriage. They want to enjoy the sense of economic freedom and to buy certain things of their own without depending on any person. These are all some reasons for getting into a job on the part of women. Employment is a substitute for dowry. In the case of women, social security is that they should be married and a suitable bridegroom can be obtained by having a job especially in the case of middle class families.

Better education and the advancement of knowledge are taken together to measure the contribution made by investment in human resources to the growth of output. It is estimated that in the annual rate of growth of a nation, nearly two-fifths can be attributed to investments in human resources. The correlation between education and productivity was found to be positive by Professor Galenson and Dr. Pyatt.

WOMEN WORKERS AND TRADE UNIONISM

The number of women workers is likely to increase with the pace of time even more because of the likely development of light industries, which cannot but employ women labour. Similarly, the number of women workers is increasing in the professions like teaching and medical institutions. Incidentally, the most suitable jobs for women so far have been teaching and nursing. Trade unions have a responsibility to see that adequate facilities are available for women workers. The membership of women workers in the trade unions is not very encouraging on account of the following.

1. The women workers are mostly uneducated and untrained.
2. Women workers have to look after their domestic work and children. This leaves hardly any energy or time with them to attend to any other work.
3. Due to some social and religious traditions, women workers even the educated ones, do not find themselves capable of mixing with male workers and inactively participate in the union activities.

The Labour Bureau, Ministry of Labour, Government of India, made a survey of the socio-economic conditions of workers in 87 units of mines of coal, iron ore limestone, a few years back. While referring to their unionisation, the survey report mentioned that with dual responsibility of family and employment, married women were generally and limestone, a few years back. While referring to their unionisation, the survey report mentioned that with dual responsibility of family and employment, married women were generally left with no leisure time except holidays. It was reported that 52 per cent women were in trade unions, but no woman was working as office-bearer or holding a responsible position. A pilot study conducted in 1981 showed that very few women were in white-collar jobs and in trade unions.

Nevertheless, it need not be emphasised that women should organise themselves. An employment prospects for women are increasing and as social values are changing, more and more women would seek more work and higher wages. It is, therefore, essential that there should be strong women's organisation and the active participation of women workers in the trade unions. Only organised and determined efforts can convert the present frustration among the women to gainful employment., to a state of complete independence with the relevance of all the social laws as in the statute books for protecting their rights and privileges.

Mass media are important instruments of the magic multiplier in social mobilisation, the process by which old socio-economic and psychological commitments are eroded and through which people become amenable to new patterns of socialisation and behaviour.

5

WOMEN AND SOCIAL LEGISLATION IN INDIA

Dr. Sudhir Chandra Jena

While women represent half of the global population and one-third of the labour force, they receive only one-tenth and less than one per cent of world property. Former U.N. Secretary-General, Kurt Waldheim in his report to the U. N. Commission on the status of women[1] had pointed out that women were responsible for two-thirds of total working hours In the Third World countries, women are responsible for more than 50% of the total production. In the African continent, women are engaged in 60 to 80 per cent of agricultural work, 50% of animal husbandry and 100% of food processing. In industrialised and advanced countries, women get only one-half to three-quarters of what men earn for the same jobs. They are categorised in lower paying female intensive jobs.[2] Further, while general illiteracy rate is falling, the female illiteracy rate is increasing, and today two out of every three illiterates are women. Therefore, through out the world, women are being discriminated. In this article, an attempt has been made to discuss the plight of Indian women in context to the social laws made so far.

In the decades after Independence, there have been tremendous historical changes in the status and position of women in Indian society. In fact, in no period of history, such revolutionary changes took place as they are taking place today. The change from a position of utter degradation in the 19th century to a position of equality in the middle of the 20th century is not a simple case of progress of women in modern India.

The women, however, in the pre-Vedic age appeared to have enjoyed a comparatively higher status than enjoyed by her sisters in the post-Vedic age.[3] In *Manusmruti*[4], for the first time, certain restrictions for women were prescribed, and from that period women were considered to be protected and thus, enjoyed a status of inequality in society. With the invasion of Turks and Persians, the position of women became deteriorated. They were pushed into *purdha* due to the fear of torture and exploitation. This not only restricted her physical movement but also affected her participation in all socio-economic activities. Polygamy came to have its way. The practice of early marriage appeared to be encouraged. Reason for early marriage was to prevent girls from entering into monastic life since many young women renounced their homes being inspired by Jainism and Buddhism.

Kuppuswamy[5] writes that since women were not educated, early marriage became common. During this period, the *purdah* also became a practice with the royal families. Widowhood became a curse in society. Widow had to bear torture by the family members as well as by the community. The practice of *Sati*, prohibition of remarriage of widow, the spread of *purdah* system and polygamy made her position very deplorable. Neera Desai[6] states that ideologically woman was considered a completely inferior species, inferior to the male, having no significance, no personality. Socially, she was kept to a state of utter subjection, denied any right, suppressed and oppressed.

Significant changes occurred in the social, economic and political status of women during the 19th century and early 20th century. There were three factors which brought these changes relating to the status of women.

1. Acceptance of tenets of liberal philosophy of the West.
2. Service of the social reformers like Raja Rammohun Roy, Dayananda Saraswati, Iswar Chandra Vidyasagar, M.G. Ranade, Keshab Chandra Sen and many others for the cause of women in India.
3. Leaders of National Movement and particularly, Gandhiji felt that liberation of the country was impossible without the active participation of women who constituted nearly half of the total population of the country.

The Indian National Congress, for the first time, passed a resolution on fundamental rights as early as 1931, which stated, "All citizens are equal before the law irrespective of caste, creed or sex."

The National Planning Committee formed under the Indian National Congress also passed a similar resolution, which runs as follows:

1. In a planned society, women's place shall be equal to that of men. Equal status, equal opportunities and equal responsibilities shall be the guiding principles to regulate the status of women.
2. Women shall not be excluded from any sphere of work merely on the ground of her sex.
3. Marriage shall not be a condition precedent to the enjoyment of full and equal civil status and economic rights by women.

After World War II, in 1945, the United Nations accepted the position of equality between men and women. Article 1 of the UN Charter seeks to achieve international cooperation in solving problems of economic, social, cultural or human character in promoting and encouraging respect for human rights and fundamental freedom for all without distinction of race, sex, language or religions etc. India was an original signatory of the UN Charter and therefore, India accepted the principle of equality and freedom for all its citizens. This has been reflected in the Preamble of the Constitution of India, which emphasised to secure to all its citizens social, economic and political justice; equality of status and opportunity; liberty of thought, expression, belief, faith and worship, and to promote among them fraternity assuring the dignity of individual.

Social legislation is the culmination of social reforms and social change based on compulsions. Where social action fails in building up a social system through the process of social education, social legislation tries to enforce action by the authority of law. During the British regime, an attempt was made to improve the situation of women in India through legislation. Some of these social laws were as follows:

1. Regulation No. XXI of 1795 and Regulation No. III of 1805 (Practice of infanticide became illegal).
2. Bengal Sati Regulation of XVII of 1829
3. Sati System Act, 1829, (Sati system became illegal).
4. The Hindu Widow's Remarriage Act, 1856.
5. Indian Penal Code, 1860, (Punishment for various offences against women like rape, adultery, bigamy, cruelty and cheating against women).
6. The Converts Marriage Dissolution Act, 1866.
7. Indian Divorce Act, 1869.
8. Special Marriage Act, 1872.
9. The Married Women's Property Act, 1874.
10. The Power of Attorney Act, 1882.
11. Civil Procedure Code, 1908, (Prohibition of arrest or detention of women in civil prison in execution of a decree for the payment of money).
12. The Legal Practitioners (Women) Amendment Act, 1923, (No women can be disqualified from being

admitted as a legal practitioner by reason of her sex).

13. Indian Succession Act, 1925, (Women have same right to property as the husband has on the death of his wife.).
14. The Child Marriage Restraint Act, 1929.
15. Arya Marriage Validity Act, 1937.
16. Hindu Widow's Right on Property Act, 1937.
17. Employment of Children (female) Act, 1938.

In post-independent period, the Constitution itself was framed with the goals of providing equality, liberty, rights and justice to all its citizens. Further, India declared herself a welfare nation to promote socio-economic well-being of all its citizens. To realise these goals, the Constitution empowers the state to make special provisions for women and children. In Chapter III of the Constitution, the following provisions are made.

1. Prohibition of traffic in human beings and forced labour. (Arts. 23-24).
2. Prohibition of discrimination on grounds of religion, race, caste, sex or place of birth. (Art. 14).
3. Equality of opportunity in matters relating to public employment. (Art.16)

Further, the Directive Principles of State Policy instructs the state to take the following welfare measures for all of its citizens.

1. Equal pay for equal work for both men and women, (Art.39d).
2. Men and women have the equal rights to an adequate means of livilihood, (Art.39a).
3. Provision of just and humane conditions of work and maternity relief, (Art.42).

4. Duty of the state to raise the level of nutrition and the standard of living and to improve public health, (Art.47).

These special provisions for women in Indian Constitution were the result of social reform movements, which began in the 19th century emphasising improvement of women's status. On the basis of these constitutional provisions, the following social laws were enacted in the post-independent India.[8]

1. Hindu Marriage Act, 1955 (Amended in 1976).
2. Hindu Succession Act, 1956 (Amended in 1986).
3. Hindu Adoption and Maintenance Act, 1956 .
4. The Suppression of Immoral Traffic in Women and Girls Act, 1956 (Amended in 1978 and 1986).
5. Hindu Minority and Guardianship act, 1956.
6. Dowry Prohibition Act, 1961 (Amended in 1984 and 1986)
7. Maternity Benefit Act, 1961 (Amended in 1976).
8. The Special Marriage Act, 1965.
9. The Medical Termination of Pregnancy Act, 1971.
10. The Factories Act, 1976.
11. The Equal Remuneration Act, 1976.
12. The Child Marriage Restraint (Amendment) Act, 1976.
13. Criminal Law (Amendment) Act, 1984.
14. The Family Courts Act, 1984
15. Indecent Representation of Women (Prohibition) Act, 1986.
16. The Sati (Prevention) Act, 1987.
17. Female Children Labour Act,
18. Immoral Traffic Prevention Act, 1986.
19. Seventy-second Amendment Act, 1992.[9]

However, in practice, the impact of these progressive laws on the status of women remains doubtful. Largely, people are unaware of these laws, or they are reluctant to change their life-style. Similarly, provisions of various social laws remain ineffective in practice as either women are not aware of these provisions, or they are not anxious to assert their rights against established norms or practices. Any empirical enquiry about the efficacy of these legal provisions relating to women, reveal that they are too radical in context of social reality and traditions.[10]

These constitutional and legal provisions should thus be analysed in context to prevailing social reality. In most Indian communities, birth of a female child is still treated as a curse and a financial liability. Currently also, demographic result of amniocentesis test on sex ratio of population has yet to be studied scientifically.[11]

The traditional Indian social structure is heavily tilted in favour of men, giving them all the authority and prestige and reducing women to the lowest status, confining to kitchen.[12] Traditional values and behavioural norms bred through thousands of years, inhibit women from asserting themselves as individuals with their independent identity and dignity. Patterns of authority prevailing in the family and society at large seem to be playing crucial role in the development of individual attitudes and orientations towards society and political system.[13]

Traditional values also restrict mobility of girls to a great extent, which in turn create hindrances in availing opportunities of learning and self-development for them. Equal education for women is hampered by a whole set of mutually dependent socio-cultural norms and traditions. The lack of educational facilities in rural areas, coupled with the view that boys are future bread-earners and should therefore, be educated first, are responsible for the illiteracy of many girls.

Pursuit of a profession by a woman requires legitimacy

to some extent, as a result of fulfillment of economic necessity. However, that has not yet led to far-reaching ideological and structural changes in the family and society. This situation is precarious for working women, who are expected to contribute to the maintenance of the family, but at the same time they are expected to fulfil all family duties and abide by the rules of sex segregation at the work place.[14]

From the above discussion, we find that there is a large gap between the enactment and enforcement of social laws for women. Moreover, different system of personal laws for different communities existing in India has widened the gap between women specially those belonging to minority communities. The problem also arises out of the fact that the government does not want to hurt the feelings of the minority community, despite public reactions against this trend. Even if, there are legal provisions for conferring the right to property to women, their position has not yet changed because of the legal provisions and the social practices, particularly in relation to the custom of dowry.

Regarding the working class women[15], there is a continued and systemic lacuna in the provisions of these Acts, some of which have already become outdated. This fact coupled with the ignorance of laws, inadequate enforcement measures and absence of enlightened employers have created problems for women at work. According to Ogburn, culture may be materialistic or non-materialistic. Materialistic culture includes man-made or visible things, where as the non-materialistic culture refers to the attitudes, beliefs, morality etc. He further says that, social change takes place due to change in cultural elements. Changes in the materialistic culture take place rapidly, while the non-materialistic culture changes very slowly. Our country is in a traditional stage, caught between traditionality and modernity. The deep-rooted traditional values and norms pose a tough resistance to the implementation of laws, creating many problems and challenges.

On 8th and 9th March, 1988, the Joint Women's Programme, a women's organisation of New Delhi organised a two-day seminar on "Economic and Property Rights for Women" in order to celebrate International Women's Day.[16] In this Seminar, Dr. Latika Sarkar pointed out that women could secure their rights only when they would achieve economic independence. Smt. C.P. Sujaya, Joint Secretary, Department of Women and Child Development felt that even in official documents women's economic contribution was drastically under-valued. This clearly reflects a gender bias and tends to make women's domestic labour invisible. She dispelled the misconception that women's income was merely a supplementary income, in fact, it was not crucial to the total family income. She called for recognition of household works undertaken by women.

Ms. Rama Devi, Member-Secretary, Law Commission pleaded for doing away with the areas of discrimination found in the Personal Laws of different religions. Only a common Civil Code could put an end to discrimination against women. Dr. Sharadamoni of Indian Statistical Institute regretted that though women made substantial contribution in the field of agriculture, they were left out in the training scheme in the new technology and its application to the agricultural sector.

On 8th March 1986, the Central Social Welfare Board also organised a seminar at New Delhi. In this seminar, Ms. Chandramani Chopra [17] suggested for the Family Courts to resolve disputes between husband and wife. Further, she said that, such Courts should be manned by experienced judicial officers, qualified social workers and counselors trained to resolve such disputes. The facts and the background of the dispute between the spouses should be enquired into by the Counselor who should report to the Court. Finally, Courts are required to go into such cases as marriage, disharmony, custody of children, maintenance, inheritance and succession. Justice S. Bhandare of Delhi High Court, in this seminar, highly criticised the diversity of personal laws. The basic reason for such wide gap between the ideal and practical in our country was partly due to historical reasons. She traces the indignity suffered by women to the social attitudes rooted in the very psyche of human beings, according to which one preferred boys to girls even in matters of education and health. The deep-seated bias cololured every thinking, attitude, action, and even, the enactment of laws and their implementation.

However, the gap between ideals and practicals should be minimised in India only when women enjoy dignity and status in society even for their being home-makers, which is in no way, socially less significant and economically less valuable than any formal occupation outside homes. People's attitude towards women should be changed. They have to give up their age-old prejudices against women through social education and exposure to mass media. Parents in rural areas should be educated to accept girls as assets and treat them without any discrimination.

The inherent nature of many social laws is confusing and sometimes, contradictory. Some alterations should be made in these laws. People's participation, especially female participation, is to be encouraged for the successful implementation of laws. Education for women is very essential for their development and improvement of status. Special emphasis should be given to legal education, in order to teach them about their legal rights, even at high school level. The legal aid should be provided to women to fight for their rights. More Family Courts should be established for certain delicate and emotional disputes for smooth disposal. Economic independence for girls is another factor to be considered and trade unions as well as women's organisations have to play an important role in this regard. These voluntary organisations should be encouraged in counselling and mediating in the disputes concerning women. They can also assist the judiciary by providing the required social data. Finally, the laws should be based on the principles of justice and equality. A determined and committed enforcement agency should be there to implement these laws in the true spirit. A system of judiciary, which interprets these to enable effective delivery of justice, should be there.

In conclusion, it can be said that, the Constitution of India and specially, the Fundamental Rights and Directive Principles of State Policy provide for equality, right and justice for women in India. On the basis of the provisions of the Constitution several laws concerning the equality, rights and development of women were enacted by the Union Parliament as well as by the State Legislatures. But, these legislation have come to limited help to women due to the conservative society, permeation of deep-rooted social evil customs, ignorance of women about social legislation and last but not the least, because of the callousness and indifference of the implementing authority. Hence, there is a need of concerted effort at all levels and by all the people for uplift of women in Indian society.

REFERENCES

1. Quoted in Agarwal, Sushila (ed.), 1988, *Status of Women*, Printwell Publishers, Jaipur, India, Introduction, pp.x-xi.
2. *Ibid.*
3. Altekar, A.S., 1962, *The Position of Women in Hindu Civilisation*, Motilal Banarasidass, New Delhi.
4. *Manusmriti*, Sloka 3:9
5. Kuppuswamy, B. 1982, *Social Change in India*, Vikas Publishing House, New Delhi.
6. Desai, Neera, 1967, *Women in Modern India*, Vora, Bombay.
7. Mishra, Saraswati, 1993, "Social Justice for Women" in *Social Welfare*, Vol. XXXIX, No.11-12, Feb.- March, pp. 12-13.
8. Department of Women and Child Development, Government of India, New Delhi.
9. Manikyamba, P., 1989, *Women in Panchayati Raj Structures*, Gian Publishing House, Delhi, p.32.

10. Ramanamma, A., 1979, *Graduate Employed Women in India in an Urban* Setting, Dastane Ramchandra and Co., Poona, p.114.
11. Chhachi, Amrita and Sathyamala, 1982, "A World without Women", *Hindustan Times*, 8th August.
12. Sirsikar, V.M., 1979, "Politicisation of Women in India" in *Symbols of Power*, ed. By Vina Mazumdar, Allied Publishers Pvt. Ltd., Bombay, p.81.
13. Eckstein and Gurr, 1975, Patterns of Authority: *A Structural Basis for Political Enquiry*, John Wiley and Sons, N.Y., p.22.
14. Nies, Maria, 1980, *Indian Women and Patriarchy*, Concept Publishing Company, New Delhi, p. 165.
15. Paul Choudhury, D., 1993, "Laws that Affect Women and Children", in *Social Welfare*, Vol. XXXIX No.11-12, February-March.
16. "Economic and Property Rights of Women" in *Social Welfare*, 1988, Vol. XXXV No. 2, May, pp.14-15.
17. "Seminar on Women and Development" in *Social Welfare*, Vol. XXXIII, No.1, April, pp.2-6.

6

IDENTITY SEARCH FOR WOMEN IN INDIA AND LEGISLATION

Dr. (Mrs.) Navaneeta Rath

In India, since long back, women were considered as the oppressed section of the society and they were neglected for centuries. Structural discriminations against women and their functional roles had stunted their development in society. The patriarchal model of the society and the role expectations of women, namely, household management, nurturing the child and adapting to the nature and demands of the male-folk had kept them subjugated and supplemented to the males of the society.

However, the movement for the emancipation of women was launched as a part of the National Movement for Independence. The western educated reformists began to realise that the condition of an important segment of the society, that is the women, was quite miserable. They were treated as non-entities, who had "roles without status" and "duties without rights." During that period, it was also realised that until and unless the women were used as manpower or human resources, the Freedom Struggle would gain no momentum and would be virtually a failure. Therefore, there was a start for doorstep campaign for the liberation of women from the household drudgery to join the National Movement. In fact, women joined the Movement in large numbers, but their leadership was very marginal without any change in their status quo. The search for identity of women really started in the post-independence period, when the educated persons, the intelligentsia, the social activists and the planners of the country started rethinking the ways and means to substitute the subsidiary role of the women with a complementary one. At this juncture, emerged the crisis of "identity search" for women.

Identity basically means the self-assertion of an individual. Therefore, in searching the identity for women, the ultimate target was their emancipation from traditional conservative social customs and to give them all opportunities to assert their position in society. And for this, ensuring gender equality was thought to be the first and foremost goal to be achieved in Indian society. It was very rightly realised that woman's personality and individuality was severely engulfed by the existing institutional or structural discriminations, which were in vogue in the society. Therefore, in the post- independence period, the prime effort of the government as well as of the social activists revolved round the incorporation of certain provisions within the spectrum of the Constitution. There was also an effort for formulation of certain social laws on the basis of the constitutional provisions, which would bring women to the forefronts of the society, liberate them from their age-old bondage and ensure them equality, dignity and justice in the society.

In fact, all the constitutional provisions as well as the social laws, which were enacted with an aim to elevate the position of the women, were launched with mainly two objectives. The first one is to curb the inhuman social practices against the women and the second one is to open new avenues for women to bargain for a better position in the society. While the first one tries to sensitise the women for asserting emancipation of women from all exploitative social practices, the latter one aims at empowering them to establish their position in the society. Therefore, the concept of emancipation coupled with the concept of empowerment are now being used as means to search just and proper identity for women in India.

CONSTITUTIONAL SAFEGUARDS FOR WOMEN

So far as the constitutional provisions are concerned the Indian Constitution guarantees equal rights to both the sexes, such as right to equality, right to freedom, right against exploitation, right to freedom of religion, right to property, cultural and educational rights, and right to constitutional remedies etc. Art. 14 and 15 of the Constitution provide for equality like equality for opportunity, equality before law, equal protection of law. The Constitution clearly states that the State shall not discriminate in enjoying rights, equality and opportunity on the basis of sex. Rather, the Constitution permits special provisions in favour of women. (Sorabjee, Soli J., 1991, p.259).

Art. 39, Clause (a) provides that the state shall in particular direct its policy towards securing adequate means of livelihood to men and women equally. Clause (b) of the same article enunciates that there shall be equal pay for equal work for both men and women. Clause (c) directs that the health and strength of the workers, men and women, and of tender age children shall not be abused and that citizens shall not be forced by economic necessity to enter a vocation unsuited to their age and strength. Thus, Art. 39 is a safeguard for the women as it intends to banish discriminations against women, and to make provisions for equal access and equal treatment of women.

Further, the Constitution of India makes it obligatory for the states under Art. 42 to make endeavours to secure just and humane conditions of work and maternity relief. Thus, it tries to safeguard women against exploitation. Art. 51 A (e) of the Constitution of India imposes it as a fundamental duty that every citizen of India shall renounce the practices derogatory to the dignity of women. Art. 325 and 326 provide equal political right to women by introducing universal adult franchise principle for the purpose of choosing representatives to decision-making bodies of the country.

Thus, the Constitution of India makes vast provisions for the protection of women and promotion of their status with the ultimate aim of ensuring a just and proper identity to women in Indian society. However, it was soon felt that the constitutional provisions would simply have no implications and would remain in a documentary form if they would not get a boost by the legal provisions. Hence, on the basis of constitutional provisions, a number of social legislations were enacted by the Parliament and the State legislatures from time to time to present a better status to women and to solve the problem of "identity crisis' for them. The entire gamut of women-specific legislation falls into three different categories, namely, social, economic and political.

SOCIAL LEGISLATION FOR WOMEN

In the post-independence period, the policy-planners, social activists and the intelligentsia strongly felt that loss of identity of women in India was an off-shoot of the social institutions, social processes and above all the social structure which were negatively conditioned towards the women and were excessively tilting towards male chauvinism. Male supremacy not only dominated the social system but also created social ambivalence for which the question of separate identity of women did not arise. Therefore, a number of social laws were enacted in the post-independence period to reduce the sense of inferiority towards women and to generate self-confidence among them.

Of all the social laws, the Special Marriage Act of 1954 and the Hindu Marriage Act of 1955 need special mention. Both these Acts created a revolutionary provision for women giving them freedom to select their own partners, if they had attained the age of 18 years. These Acts allowed women to select their mates even from outside their own caste, sub-caste, community and religion, if they so choose. They were also accorded with the option to resort to civil marriage, which does not require any customary ceremonies accompanied by rituals. These provisions are no doubt, a great challenge to the restricted voice of girls which was long subjugated by their parental options coupled with caste endogamy and religious taboos. By hiking the age of marriage, the Marriage Acts tried to put an end to the practice of child marriage which resulted in early widowhood, early motherhood and increased number of maternal as well as infant mortality. However, the Hindu Marriage Act of 1955 was amended in 1978 under the title of The Child Marriage Restrained (Amendment) Act of 1978. This Act again raised the marriageable age of girls to 18 and that of boys to 21 and made more stringent rules relating to the ban of the system of child marriage. However, now the voice is being raised from different quarters to raise the marriageable age of girls from 18 to 21, so that the girls would be more physically and mentally equipped with for safe motherhood and active citizens.

Another notable content of the Special Marriage Act of 1954 and the Hindu marriage Act of 1955 was the abolition of polygamy, which inflicted its negative consequences on the identity of the Hindu women. Both the Acts made polygamy legally void and championed the cause of monogamy. Section 5 (I) of the Hindu Marriage Act of 1955 provides that no one with a living spouse can have a second marriage. Polygamy when becomes practised by the male persons, it supports the subservient role of women. Women become easily physically as well as psychologically exploited without getting any emotional commitment from their husbands. This leads to the loss of identity of Women who do not have any claim as a wife. However; this women-related problem has been liquidated to some extent by the aforesaid two marriage Acts.

Added to these Provisions, both the Marriage Acts also laid down the criteria for designating a marriage as invalid. According to these marriage laws, a Hindu marriage will be considered as invalid on the following grounds, namely, if it is bigamy or, if either party suffers from unsound mind or mental disorder or if either party is impotent or if the boy has not completed 21 years and the girl 18 years, or, if the partners are closely related within the prohibited relationship category.

The inclusion of the provisions for declaring a Hindu marriage invalid on the aforesaid grounds no doubt, created a new chapter in the prevailing system of marriage and protected the Women from Physical and mental trouble. Besides, the existing idea that 'Hindu marriage is a religious sacrament and the marital relationship once established, continue for generations' compelled the Hindu women to accept all the adversities without any resistance. This Was undoubtedly an expression of her lack of identity and of her extreme dependence on the male partner. But the provision of divorce in the Marriage Acts provided her independence and gave recognition to her identity as a human being. The divorce provisions again ensured the right to claim maintenance from the husband depending upon his income and economic status. This again assured the woman a secured position in the family and the society.

One of the most important social legislations having its far-reaching consequences on the protection of women from atrocities and in providing them a better identity happens to be the Dowry Prohibition Act of *1961* which has later been amended several times. The Act has defined dowry as any property or valuable articles given or agreed to be given either directly or indirectly by one party to the other party at the time of marriage, or by parents of either party at or before or after the marriage as a condition of the marriage of the said parties.

However, Dowry prohibition Act of 1961 could not do

much in relation to the protection of women from the torturous practice of dowry. Dowry as a process always represented the masculine supremacy in Indian society, where the woman's identity was totally overshadowed. The sacred institution of marriage was totally perverted by this practice of dowry and the women's role in the institution of family and marriage was totally ignored.

Taking note of the seriousness and gravity of the problem of dowry and its cancerous growth on an unprecedented scale, the Parliament took various steps to plunge the loopholes in the law so as to make the provisions of law pragmatic and effective. (Gaur, K.D., 1994). In December 1980, the Parliament appointed a Joint Select Committee to examine and suggest various measures to streamline the Dowry Prohibition Act of 1961. The Committee submitted its report to Parliament in August 1982 and suggested inter alia a number of important changes of consequential significance. Accordingly, the Parliament amended the Dowry Prohibition Act of 1961 and enacted Dowry Prohibition (Amendment) Act, 1984. A number of significant provisions have been made under this Act like, the establishment of family court, cognisance of the offences under this Act, severe penalties for demanding dowry etc. Further, two important amendments have also been made in the Indian Penal Code in 1983 and 1986 respectively to handle with the crimes relating to dowry. All these laws are intended to liberate women from harassment, humiliation, torture and bride-burning.

Another important social legislation having its bearing on tracing identity for the women in India happens to be the "Hindu Adoption and Maintenance Act" of 1956. Under this Act, the Hindu wife and her children are to be maintained by her husband. A wife is given the option to live separately from her husband and claim maintenance from him, if her husband is suffering from leprosy or is guilty of cruelty, desertion, bigamy, or conversion to another religion. The wife can also claim maintenance after the break-up of marriage under the Marriage Act of 1954 and 1955.

The Maintenance Act serves as an identity saving device for thousands of women of the country who are accorded with both status and esteem at least from economic point of view after they become separated from their husbands. The age-old idea that women have no locus standing without their husbands is gradually dying out because of these social legislation.

The Hindu Adoption Act of 1956 is another landmark social legislation that dramatically altered the subordinate status of the Hindu women and adorned them with a better status. Particularly according to the Hindu social stigma, a childless woman was looked down upon by the society and had to lead a life of torture. She had no identity neither in the family, nor in the community. Contrary to this situation of woman, Adoption Act entitled the right of adoption on an unmarried, widow and a divorcee woman as well as an issueless woman.

Carrying unwanted pregnancies in case of women is another factor for lowering down the prestige of women in society. In such cases, the rehabilitation of unmarried mothers and illegitimate children become a major social problem not only for the family but also for the society. Single motherhood also brings not only social but also psychological torture for women. Considering this situation, the Indian Parliament enacted the Medical Termination of Pregnancy Act, which came into force in 1972. This legislation stipulates that, if the pregnant woman is a major, her consent for the termination of pregnancy is required. However, in some states, amniocenteses has been banned, as it leads to the killing of female foetus in mother's womb. Longing for a male child is an age-old social custom, which gives an inferior status to women and women themselves lose their confidence and self-assertion.

A widow loses her identity with the death of her husband. So there was the system of "Sati" which was another torture for a Hindu woman. This led the status of woman to marginality from which it was very difficult for her to escape. Even during the pre- independence period, the inhuman practice of *Sail* was combated with, but it was not fully abolished from Indian soil. It continued to be practices in some form or other in many parts of the country and very recently with the incidence of Roop Kanwar the issue was very hotly debated. As a result, The Government of India passed the Sati (Prevention) Act of 1987.

An important provision of the Act is the establishment of special courts for trial of offences under the Act. Clause (C) to Section 1 of the Act of 1987 defines *Sail*, "the practice of burning or burying alive any widow along with the body of her husband, or any other relative or with any article, object or thing irrespective of whether such burning or burying is voluntary on the part of the widow." Section 4 of the same Act prescribes that any person guilty of abetting Sati directly or indirectly, shall be punished with death sentence or life imprisonment or fine. Those guilty of glorifying Sati may be punished with imprisonment upto seven years and fine. Hence, this Act has given a social recognition to women, to their role, status and to their independence.

Further, in consonance with the International Convention signed at New York on May 9, 1950 for the prevention of immoral traffic of women, the Indian government enacted the Immoral Traffic (Prevention) Act of 1956. This Act has given a legal status to women by drastically banning their commercial utilisation and exploitation. In the same vein, Section 375 and 376 of the Indian Penal Code deal with the issue of rape. The Criminal Law Amendment Act of 1983 clearly spells out the punishment to the culprit for rape and thereby the Act ensures social security to women who are being physically exploited and mentally harassed due to their soft temperament and biological structure.

Another women-specific legislation is the Indecent Representation of Women (Prohibition) Act of 1986. This Act prohibits the derogatory representation of women through advertisements or in publications, writings, paintings, figures or in any other manner and for matters connected therewith or incidental thereto. This is obviously a commendable attempt to elevate the position of women and to locate her in a prestigious position in society.

Finally, to ensure speedy justice to the women in family disputes, the Indian government enacted The Family Courts Act in 1984. The Act prescribes for the establishment of Family Courts to promote conciliation in and secure speedy settlement of disputes relating to marriage and family affairs and for matters connected therewith.

However, since the beginning of the Sixth Five Year Plan period, the Government realised that women's identity can not be traced only in the constitutional provisions or in the social legislations. Identity can be best located when women would be treated as a major component in the developmental network of the country. Identity has to be achievement-based. The achievement of the women can be judged when they would have greater and better role in the economy or in the production unit. But their role in the production unit should be converted from unskilled to skilled producers. To bring about such a new role for the women, the government felt the need of enunciation of new policies specifically for women with a view to empower them and to assert their status in the society. In this context, the education policies of the government need special mention.

EDUCATION POLICIES FOR WOMEN

Education has all along been treated as the major instrument that can promote equality among women and can empower them. However, for a long time education was considered as a male sector and women were deprived of education. So the National Government adopted the Universal Primary Education policy to provide free primary education to all upto fourteen years of age and to make the educational sector gender- neutral. In some states like Orissa, girls education has become free up to the completion of university education. Accordingly, the government had tried to modernise the school text-books and to make them gender-neutral. On the other hand, the government is trying to give new identity to women through text-book syllabus by presenting the greater and important roles performed by the ancestral women in Indian society. The government has opened a number of girls' schools and institutions to bring more and more women to the fold of education. In order to give incentives to girl students, in many states women education even in higher stages has become free and a number of scholarship provisions are made for them. Reservation of seats for the women candidates in various educational institutions has also been made by the government in some states to drag more and more women to the purview of higher education and professional training. Regional vocational training institutes, industrial training institutes and polytechnic centres for exclusively women are set up by the state governments in some states to provide training facilities to them in the basic, advanced and institutional level skills. Kanyashrams are set up in villages to provide residential facilities to the tribal girls in tribal areas and to promote education among them. Finally, the Government of India with the assistance of the World Bank has identified the girls as "The Doubly Disadvantaged Groups" and special efforts are being geared to educate them under the call of "Education for All by 2000 A.D.".

ECONOMIC POLICIES FOR WOMEN

The government at the centre as well as in the states

soon became aware that the social and educational policies for women would have no yield unless and until they are coupled with some broad economic policies. The location of women in the frontlines of the economic scenario of the country would necessarily render them a distinct identity. The basic goal of the economic policies relates to the development of women as a major human capital or resource, whereby women would be economically self-reliant and thus empowered.

The Mahila Samridhi Yojana (MSY) is one of the leading economic policies for women. It gives coverage to seventy per cent of the total rural women in India. The objective of this programme is to sensitise the women about their role in the economic sector of the country and to cultivate a habit of thrift among them. Under this scheme, rural women are encouraged to save when they are provided with direct cash incentives to supplement their individual savings. Similarly, National Credit Fund (NCF) or Mahila Kosh is targetted towards the economic uplift of women of the country, whether rural or urban. It is a flexible women-friendly project, which backs and supports the women to become self-reliant and generate in them a spirit of economic participation through the easy availability of credit to them.

The government to bring women to the fold of economic empowerment is launching several employment and income generating schemes. Once she starts to contribute to the income flow of the family, her status becomes totally elevated. Employment of women in formal sectors is the single alternative that can cut across the socio-economic disparities between men and women and which can solve the identity crisis of women. In some states like Orissa, the state government has made reservations for women in the government jobs. The government has also made age relaxation for the women to enter into government jobs. In various employment-generation schemes launched by the government women have become the target group. For developing the entrepreneurial skills among women, the government is providing Enterpreneurship Development Training to the women. Women can easily get loans from nationalised banks for agriculture and for starting any other income generating schemes. The government has also established the Mahila Banks and the Mahila Vikas Samabaya Nigams for making easy credit provisions for women and for making provisions for their self-employment.

LEGISLATION FOR WOMEN IN POLITICAL SPHERE

Women should not only be the subjects, but they should participate in the decision- making bodies, if they want to be really empowered and possess an identity of their own. Development needs participation of citizens not only in enjoying the benefits of development, but also in participating in the decision for identifying the needs, the fixation of goals, determination for achieving those goals and mobilisation of resources etc. Participation in decision-making bodies refers to participation in politics, which is so far considered a male's sphere in Indian society. In order to give opportunities to women *to* enter into politics, the 73rd and 74th Amendment of the Constitution has been made in 1992 and 33% of reservation of seats in Local Bodies, both urban and rural, has been made for women. This is just the first attempt of government to offer a political identity to women by dragging them more in number to the fold of decision-making bodies. However, steps are being taken to reserve seats for women in the Parliament and the State legislatures.

CONCLUSION

It can be undoubtedly said that most numerous and important legislation for women are made in India compared to other countries of the world. These laws are all embracing in character and are expected to have cast a significant influence on the women Community. But, the real scene differs much from the prescribed one. There is a wide gap between the intentions and the performance. In fact, the laws are successful in giving positive results in certain spheres, particularly, so far as the urban and elite women arc concerned. But the laws remain only as letters on paper for the ruralite, uneducated common class women who outnumber the former class. And for this, poverty, ignorance, unawareness, social customs and taboos and unwillingness to develop on the part of women themselves are responsible. The governmental machinery and NGOs are also becoming callous and lethargic in implementing the legislation for women. Therefore, the concepts of emancipation, equality and empowerment have not made much headway and identity crisis for women remains a continuing problem not only for women as a class but for the society at large. To make laws cannot be said tò be the be-all and end-all to solve this problem of identity crisis for women. Proper implementation of such laws, their percolation to the grass-roots level and above all mass mobilisation and a conscious effort on the part of all the citizens - male and female- can only solve the prolonged issue of identity crisis for women in Indian society.

REFERENCES

Ahuja, Ram, 1992, *Rights of Women: A Feminist Perspective,* Rawat Publications, Jaipur.

Gangrade, K.D., 1978, *Social Legislations in India* , Vol.1 and Vol.2, Concept Publishing Company, Delhi.

Gaur, K.D., 1994, "The Poor Woman: Victim of Dowry, Bride Burning a Socio Economic Malady : Need for Introspection" O.C. Sharma, (ed.), *Crime Against Women,* Ashish Publishing House.

Sorabjee, Soli J., 1991, "Women, Constitution and the Courts" in Shamduddin Sham (ed.), *Law and Social Change,* Ashish Publishing House, New Delhi

Subhramanyam, K., 1991, *Women and Law,* Asia Law House, Hyderabad.

7

WOMEN'S DEVELOPMENT: FROM A GRASS-ROOT DEVELOPMENT PERSPECTIVE (GRDP)

Dr.(Mrs.) Sharada Rath

"Development" as a concept has got new and operational meanings, approaches and dimensions not only in the developed countries, but also in the third world countries which are on the way of development. Key elements in the development approaches are awareness, interest, involvement and empowerment of individual, of the groups and of the communities. There is a shift of focus in the development administration from production-centred approach to the people-centred approach, which needs that the people should not be viewed as a subject only but as an actor who can define the goals, control the resources, and direct the process affecting his or her life.

No development programme can be successful in India unless it is seen from grassroots development perspectives. This is due to the fact that the soul of India lies in villages, as Mahatma Gandhi said during the National Movement and this is also true today, when more than two-thirds of the people live in rural areas. Therefore, rural development constitutes an inseparable and necessary component of the national development process.

However, no rural development can be conceived of

ignoring the development of the women who constitute half of the rural population but enjoy an unequal, differentiated and lower socio-economic status. In fact, the mention of women's development opens a Pandora's box of complex problems. Due to the pluralistic, diversified and stratified nature of society, development of women in India is indeed, an uphill task. Nevertheless, it is true that status of urban women has been changed perceptibly in the post-independence India. Exposure of women to formal education and participation in labour force have brought out changes in the role and status of urban women. (Rita Sood, 1991).

In this paper, an attempt has been made to find out how rural women and grassroots development are linked in India. Grassroots approach to development can be better discussed by putting emphasis on three points, namely, (1) proper identification of potentialities of rural women; (2) proper demarcation of their basic needs; and (3) enabling the women beneficiaries to be involved in implementation of the programme. GRDP implies the change and development policies specifically meant and determined by the group of women for whom development policies are made. This approach is different from "mainstream" approach which is more holistic and more general to be applied for all women ignoring the differences of the potentialities and basic needs of the particular groups of women. As Archana Kalegaon Kar (1997) has rightly pointed out that key to grassroots approach is not the provision of a particular set of needs but rather the *process* by which they are satisfied. Thus, women development from GRDP should identify the potentialities, articulate the basic needs of women and enable them to implement the developmental programmes for themselves.

In context to the status of women, two parallel trends of thinking have gained prominence in the past two decades: One is the women and development debate and the other is the feminist movement debate. (Mukta Mittal, 1995). In case of rural women in India, the former has always taken the lead over the latter on the basic assumption that socio-economic development would lead to mobilisation as well as the liberation of women from subjugation and subordination in society. "Equality" is the catchword of women's development theory in India and "more than equal" is the feminist theory which has not yet attracted the attention of the scholars in case of rural women.

Again, there is a shift in development discourses from "Women in Development" (WID) to "Gender and Development" (GAD) because of the relative lack of focus on the "self-empowerment" of women within the institutional framework of the WID. In the WID approach, women are only integrated / incorporated into the development process. In contrast, GAD emphasises the autonomy and independence of women over their lives. In this sense, they become agents of their own development, and are able to exercise choices and set their own agendas. Conceptually, woman is a biological category and gender is a social category. Gender is not an isolated category: it is a social relation between men and women. Socially constructed asymmetrical relationship (with woman in a subordinating role) has always been addressed in the gender approach.

RURAL WOMEN AND DEVELOPMENT: NEW DIMENSIONS

Coming to the rural women in India, the basic principles of women development are identified as welfare, equity, anti-poverty, efficiency and empowerment. (Moser, Caroline O.N. 1993). Once speaking at the special session of International Labour Conference in Geneva, late Rajiv Gandhi, the then Prime Minister of India spoke on the agenda of reforms for women and spelt out the priorities of his government in these words: "The economic and social emancipation of women ranks high on our agenda. The totality of their welfare, equal access to education, equal wages, maternity and child benefits, special health care, the ending of socially discriminatory practices, all this will claim our attention and resources, and will make their social status". The Fourth World Conference on Women in Beijing in 1995 had also discussed and adopted "A Platform for Action" on twelve critical areas of concern which stand in the way of women's development the world over with poverty topping the list. However, Government of India has made serious efforts to ensure a better status to women, to utilise their untapped potential for national development, and as such, to bring them to the mainstream of the process of development. To attain this goal, the Government has adopted a multi-dimensional approach of providing education, ensuring health services, creating opportunities of income-generating work; fostering orientation and attitude conducive to development as well as accelerating the participation of the women in the development programmes.

The concept of "empowerment" of rural women is a recent step taken by the government which implies positive action and participatory role of women in the decision-making bodies. Empowerment does not mean only the women's liberation from patriarchal institutions but it implies the development of women in all spheres - intellectual, moral, political , and socio-economic. It is always construed in the context of the concept of "autonomy". The purpose of using "autonomy" as a strategy is to generate some social space in which women can maneuver and achieve powers over their own lives and over their socio-cultural realities. "Autonomy" implies power in the sense of one's capacity to define his/her own agenda. It is an emancipatory strategy, and addresses the issues of self-determination. It presupposes serious questioning of gender arrangements and the varying social hierarchies and distances present in a society and implies democratic, emancipatory, and redistributive mechanisms.

However, "Power" is a human construct which can not be given to one as alms but, which is to be claimed and acquired by one. For that women of the rural areas are to be "emancipated" and "developed". "Empowerment" has got no meaning if there would be no emancipation of women from household drudgery and development of women through welfare measures. Women's development is inextricably tied to women's liberation from patriarchal institutions and to their active role in nation-building.

Emancipation of women in rural areas had already been started with Gandhiji's clarion call for women for joining the National Movement. This was the first effort for emancipation of women in India and under Gandhiji's leadership, many rural women in India stepped out of their homes and took a very active part in Indian liberation movement. However, the percentage of rural women to urban women in India joining the National Movement was marginal and as soon as the country became independent the emancipation of rural women got a setback.

THE CONSTITUTION, LEGISLATIONS AND WOMEN IN INDIA

The adoption of the Constitution in 1950 is a landmark in the history of progress and development of women in India. The Constitution makes no distinction on the basis of sex and provides rights, freedom and privileges equally to both men and women. The Preamble of the Constitution promises to secure to all its citizens justice, liberty, equality and fraternity. To attain these constitutional objectives, the Constitution guarantees certain fundamental rights and freedom such as freedom of speech, protection of life and personal liberty. On the one hand, the Constitution ensures "equality before law", and on the other it, "prohibits any discrimination" on the basis of sex. Special provision for women has been made in Art. 15(3) of the Constitution which marks the violation of the fundamental obligation of non-discrimination among citizens, inter-alia of sex. This provision has enabled the state to make special provisions for women, particularly in the field of labour legislations like the Factories

Act and Mines Act and provisions for reservation of seats in decision-making bodies like Panchayats. Directive Principles of the Constitution concern women directly and have a special bearing on their status. These include Art. 39(a) (Right to adequate means of livelihood for men and women equally); (d) (equal pay for equal work both for men and women); (e) (protection of health and strength of workers - men, women and children) and Art. 42 (Just and humane conditions of work and maternity relief) and reservation of seats for women in Panchayat institutions (73rd Amendment of the Constitution, 1992).

On the basis of these constitutional provisions, a number of social legislations have been made both by the national government and the state governments to elevate the status of women. Amongst these, the important legislations concerning the status of women are Marriage Act, Hindu Marriage Act, Hindu Succession Act, Hindu Adoption and Maintenance Act, Hindu Minority and Guardianship Act, Dowry Prohibition Act, Women's and Children's Institution (Licensing)Act, Medical Termination of Pregnancy Act, and Anti-rape Laws. But the problem for rural women is that they know very little about these women-related constitutional provisions and the social legislations. Lack of education, undeveloped socio-economic condition and lack of proper socialisation are responsible for the ignorance of the rural women about their constitutional rights and obligations.

PLANNING AND DEVELOPMENT PROGRAMMES FOR RURAL WOMEN

Since the beginning of planning in India, the welfare and development of women attracted the attention of the planners. The concept of "development" superseded the concept of "emancipation", so far as the problems of women were concerned. Nehru himself had written, "If I may be allowed to pay greater stress on some, they would be the welfare of the children, the status of women and the welfare of the tribal and hilly people of our country". In the first four plan periods (1952-1974), the approach of the government was to focus women as targets of welfare policies in the social sector. In the Fifth and Sixth Plan, there was a shift in the government's approach from "welfare" to "development" with a definite thrust on health, education and employment. In all these programmes, attention was paid and is being paid even today to bring more and more women into the fold of development. 30% of the beneficiaries under IRDP are to be the women and therefore, NABARD has advised not to ask from rural women any collateral security or third party guarantee for loans under IRDP upto the limit of Rs. 10,000/- for agriculture and allied activities and Rs.25,000/- for other activities. NABARD has further given instructions that bank assistance under IRDP should not be denied to women only because ownership of land and other properties are not registered in their names. Under TRYSEM 33% of reservation has been made for women beneficiaries. DWCRA is meant specially for women in rural areas, where rural women should be encouraged to form working groups so that they can take up income-generating activities and become self-reliant. Government has launched Universal Literacy Programme, emphasis being placed on the rising trend of the enrolment of girl-child as well as on the reduction of their drop-out rates. Hence, Lower Primary, Upper Primary and High Schools are established by the government in different rural areas. To provide medical facilities to rural women, a number of dispensaries with doctors, nurses, midwives and medicines are provided by the government under the programme, "Health for All". Efforts were also made to improve the status of women through economic planning process. For the first time a separate chapter on "Women and Development" was included in the Sixth Five Year Plan. More attention was paid to the conditions of women in the Seventh Five Year Plan and important strategies were discussed in the Plan document.

The Seventh Plan proclaimed : "The long-term objectives of the developmental programmes for women would be to raise their economic and social status in order to bring them into the mainstream of national development. Due recognition has to be accorded to the role and contribution of women in the various socio-economic, political and cultural activities". The Eighth plan (1992-97) laid special thrust on employment including women's employment with the objective to make women self-reliant and economically independent. Rashtriya Mahila Kosh is the most significant intervention launched in 1993 with the objective of meeting the credit needs of the poor, assetless women mostly in the informal sector.

Despite all these development programmes launched by the government, the response of rural women to these measures is not encouraging. Historically, rural women had been subjected to various kinds of exploitation. Educationally they are still backward. Only 13% to 15% of rural women are educated while 39% of women on national scale are being educated. Economic independence, for a majority of rural women is still a dream which constantly eludes them. (Najma Heptulla, 1992).

Interviews and informal discussions with the sample women respondents reveal that the attitude, opinion, perception and participation of rural women in the development programmes are quite apathetic. They have developed an indifferent attitude, negative opinion and a different perception for the development programmes launched by the government. Hence, the rural women beneficiaries are still remaining marginal. This raises the question : What are the causes for which the development benefits do not reach the rural women and their backwardness is still persisting sometimes causing serious bottlenecks on the path of the country's progress ?

An objective study of the women's development points out that there are two main reasons for which rural women are not getting their due benefits. These are, namely, no proper identification of potentialities of rural women has been made and secondly, no specific problems of rural women have been demarcated, while developmental policies are being made and implemented.

POTENTIALITIES OF RURAL WOMEN

The potentialities of rural women are to be identified in order to achieve the basic principles of development "welfare, equity, anti-poverty, efficiency and empowerment". Karl Waldheim, the ex-Secretary General of the United Nations had rightly pointed out, "We must think positively about how the position of women in their own societies and in international affairs could not only be improved, but their large potential contribution be better utilised for the benefit of all".

Women's potentialities as mothers, as household managers, as income-earners and as protectors of the environment are always undervalued and this has become major factor for male dominance in society. Differing biological endowments of men and women have led to subordination and subjugation of women in society. This is true not only in case of India, but also in many countries of the world. Although "the degrees and expression of female subordination vary greatly, social asymmetry is manifested in separate spheres for men and women, and the domestic sphere in which women function is consistently undervalued compared with the public sphere where men gain prestige, status, authority and value." (Rosaldo and Lamphere, 1982). Women not only give birth to children, but they raise them to full citizens who will have an active role in building the nation and the society. Women can perform these functions, only when they are properly educated and they themselves can maintain good health. A woman's education and good health are assets for the society as she is the builders of the future citizens.

Women are household managers as they have to manage the domestic activities in an efficient manner. Upon the ability, efficiency, and wisdom of women, the well-being of the family depends. Particularly in rural areas, in many families the male persons migrate to the nearby urban area to earn cash money and they come home occasionally. The burden of household management falls upon the shoulders of women. Therefore, women need education to manage the household affairs.

Rural women, in most cases, are income-earners. It is estimated that rural women earn more than the rural male-folk, as the women have to work in farms, in cottage industries, and also in selling the products in the market. Finally, rural women, particularly in forest areas, are the protectors of environment. Due to their life-long experiences and inborn instincts, they can do the job of afforestation far better and at a lower cost than many of the urban people who are associated with social forestry. Their indigenous knowledge of afforestation should be properly utilised instead of being systematically destroyed. They have been the only ones to have kept a balance between human and environmental needs. Women's potentialities in their domestic roles and biological functions are to be properly valued and they should not be related to socio-cultural arrangements, which had given rise to female subordination in society. Rather, their potentialities are to be properly understood in order to measure their general and specific needs for making public policies.

PROBLEMS OF RURAL WOMEN

The problems of rural women are different from those of male persons. The women's issues in rural areas can be categorised into three main groups, namely, socio-cultural, economic and political. Socio-culturally, women in rural areas are treated as inferior and subordinate to their male counterparts. This is partly due to age-long established tradition, superstition, worn-out customs, social beliefs, norms and unwritten taboos that have pervaded the Indian rural society for ages. The rural women had accepted their inferior and dependent status wholeheartedly and the society had also accepted the same. However, the inferior status of rural women is mostly due to the lack of female literacy in rural areas. In most cases, the school site is far away from the habitats for which the female children are not able to go to school. In some cases also the schools are not working at all, their names are on papers only. The female child in rural areas is preferred to remain at home to help her mother in household chores rather than going to schools. Female drop-out in schools is still a marked feature and female literacy in large number is yet to be achieved.

Similarly, the health condition of rural women is very poor. It has been admitted that, age-old tradition, social taboos, superstition, ignorance and poverty prevent the rural women to avail the medical facilities. They do not come to the hospital in time and only when their condition becomes serious, they come for treatment and their death becomes inevitable, even if proper treatment is given to them at their last stage. This is due to the lack of education and lack of health consciousness on the part of the rural people. Added to this are lack of adequate hospital facilities, lack of medicine, absence of lady doctors in remote areas, and no provision of mobile dispensaries which are responsible for bad health plight of rural women. Under ICDS programme, no regular health check-up is being made of women. Vaccinations are very irregular and casual. Imparting of health education to the rural women is completely absent. Proteneous diet which are being distributed to the rural women under the ICDS programmes are both rotten and inadequate. A DWCRA worker expressed that a pregnant woman gets only 160 gms. of wheat, 20 gms. of gur, 30 gms. of dal, and 15 gms. of salt which are very inadequate as proteneous food material for a pregnant mother. Again, all the pregnant women in rural areas are not getting it. Due to malnutrition, rural women suffer from anemia and anemic women in rural areas are estimated roughly to be 60% to 80%.

Economically, rural women are in a state of poverty. Rural people, in general, are poor. But rural women are poorer than the rural men. For, land and whatever savings the family possesses, that belong to the male persons. Women have little property rights. Even if rural female participation in the economic process is always higher than the total male participation and the urban female participation, their work always remains unpaid or underpaid. They do not earn cash money as they are not engaged in gainful employment in formal sectors.

In the political scene as well, the role of rural women is felt very marginally. It is rightfully stated that neither the governmental officers nor the NGOs have tried to encourage the women villagers to speak out their needs on which a new line of planning for development can be made. Further, the participatory institution in the village area is the Panchayats. Realising the low participation of rural women in these local institutions, provisions are made for reservation of seats for women in local bodies by 73rd Amendment of the Constitution, 1992. This is certainly a significant step in political empowerment of women and consequently, their participation in decision- making bodies of rural areas.

On the reservation issue, Dr. Vina Mazumdar (1979) , the leading feminist scholar of India had expressed her views relating to the logic behind putting some seats for women in the Panchayats. To her, it "seems that there is a confusion here between women as individuals and women as an interest group. The moment you say that there must be some women on a decision-making body like the Panchayat, you are in a way suggesting that there are certain problems in which women have special interests. And in order to ensure that there is a representation of those interests you have to include some women. This is the only way in which I can choose to interpret this thesis. But if this is for representation of an interest group then why are the modalities missing? How do the women come into the Panchayat? In most of the cases it is the Sarapanch's wife herself. So what you get is somebody from the already dominant group in that village coming in as a representative of women. In most of the cases none of these women have ever been told as to what their rights are or what their responsibilities are and nobody has thought of organising any kind of training programme for these women. In most of the cases that were examined we found that women are not even aware as to what they were supposed to be doing. Some papers will be sent to them and then their thumb prints will be taken. When you have this kind of representation of an interest group to a power structure which is hostile, it is ineffective."

Dr. Mazumdar's anticipation has not gone in vain. It is found that on the basis of reservation of seats in rural local bodies, women are elected to the local panchayats against their willingness and interest. Despite the presence of women, these local bodies are in reality controlled by the male persons who are more numerous and dominating due to the patriarchal nature of the society. Female participation in decision-making bodies is a farce, when the male persons run the Panchayati Raj institutions to suit themselves, no matter what the women want. Hence, the Panchayats which can act as ventilators of the needs of rural women are becoming more of male's domain and the problems of women development are least discussed in Panchayat meetings. The voluntary organisations like Mahila Samities, Cooperative Societies, Village Clubs etc. are also not effective agencies to mobilise the rural women to participate in development process. Women membership, their attendance and their participation in the meetings and activities of these non-governmental bodies in the rural areas are remaining marginal.

Suggestions for Removal of Backwardness of Rural Women

Diagnoising the disease is an important task, but it is not the sole method of curing the disease. Prescriptions based on diagnosis are necessary to cure the disease. In case of the backwardness of rural women, many plans and programmes had already been implemented by the government, but the response of the rural women to these measures are very negligible. After so many years of experimentation on implementing welfare measures for rural women, their backwardness has not been perceptibly removed and the time has now come to assess the programmes and to rethink over the policy measures to find out the lacunae in the programmes and to rectify them accordingly to make the programmes more viable, feasible, and purposive to achieve the target. Hence, following suggestions can be made for development of women from grassroots development perspective.

The potentialities of rural women should be properly identified and encouraged and not to be ignored. All development programmes should be made in consonance with the development of potentialities of rural women of a particular area. No common development programmes for women will work out, as the rural women pose a different picture from the urban women as well as the problems of tribal women are not the same as the women of the general caste. Hence, in chalking out any development programme for women, emphasis should be on indigenous problems and priorities. Therefore, planning should be decentralised upto the grassroots level. Education of rural women should be undertaken on war-footing measures, as immediate and urgent need by opening primary schools in every village and providing sufficient cost-free study materials. Monetary incentives should be given to the teachers of the rural primary schools as well as to the parents of girl child for sending their children to school. Without proper education women cannot enjoy the benefits of development nor they can participate in the process of decision-making in family, in community and in rural local bodies. Adequate health facilities including free medicines, vitamin pills, medical education, nurses, midwifes and lady doctors should be provided for women in rural areas. If women would be physically weak, they would be a liability not only for the family, but also for the community and for the nation as a whole. Periodic appraisal of the progress of rural women by the governmental agencies as well as by the non-governmental agencies is necessary. Every effort should be made to assimilate the rural women not only as the recipients of benefits of welfare measures, but as active participants in the input process of the development. It is no more proper to put the responsibility of development of women only on governmental bodies, but the home agencies like parents, husband, family members and relatives; community agencies like voluntary associations, community centres, women organisations, cooperatives, schools, teachers etc.; governmental agencies like panchayats, legislature, bureaucracy and planning bodies; and media agencies like newspaper, T.V., radio and films should hold the responsibility for development of rural women. Home agencies will help in socialisation for developing culture of equal development and participation of women; community agencies will help in developing social acceptance and individual awareness for the equal status of women; government agencies will legalise women's participation in making and implementing policies; and, media agencies will create full and equivalent exposure making of choices and building of role images of rural women. All these agencies should be active and dynamic and should work in cooperation and harmony particularly, on three counts, namely, to check corruption, to implement the policies vigorously and to motivate women to participate in decision-making.

CONCLUSION

Backwardness of rural women is not a natural but a social phenomenon having its root on social customs, traditions, and beliefs. But it is a liability for the nation as a whole. Hence, it is to be uprooted by providing equality, dignity, freedom and opportunity to empower rural women in order to be not only as efficient mothers and housewives, but as the active citizens having positive roles in the nation-building process. Women are not anti-development, but they want improvement to utilise their potentialities for better life. In the past, development programmes for the rural women have often failed, because their potentialities were not known, their needs were ignored, they were not listened to and policies were made for them by keeping them aside in the formulation stage as well as in the implementation of the programmes. But, if a "sustainable social process is to be built from below", there is the need to ensure genuine empowerment at the grassroots. The rural women have to gain a voice, access and control over social, economic and political processes that affect them. The dependence-development syndrome in case of rural women has been proved wrong and it is to be replaced by the design that rural women can develop as the starter and not as the appendages to the urban women or to the male-folk of the society.

REFERENCES

Amar, Jesani; 1990, "Limits of Employment - Women in Rural Health Care" *Economic And Political Weekly*, May 19.

Boserup, Ester, 1970, *Women's Role in Economic Development*, St. Martin's Press, New York.

Das, B.K. 1992, "Women in Rural Development : The Indian Experience" in C. Kalbagh (ed.), *Women and Development*, Discovery Publishing House, New Delhi.

Government of India, 1988, *National Perspective Plan for Women 1988-2000 A.D.*, Ministry of HRD, Department of Women & Child Development.

Hanumappa, H.G. & T.M. Sujatha, 1992, "The Changing Status of Rural Women" in C. Kalbagh, (ed.), *Women and Development.*

Heptulla, Nazma, (ed.), 1992, *Reforms for Women : Future Options,* Oxford & IBH Publishing Co. Pvt. Ltd., New Delhi.

Kar, Archana Kalegaonkar, 1997, "Pursuing Third World Women's Interests : Compatibility of Feminism with Grass Roots Development", *Economic and Political Weekly,* April 26.

Mazumdar, Vina, (ed.) 1979, Symbols of Power : *Studies on the Political Status of Women in India,* New Delhi, Allied Publishers

Mittal, Mukta (ed.), 1995, *Women Power in India,* Anmol Publications Pvt. Ltd., New Delhi, First Edition.

Moser, Caroline O.N. 1993, *Gender Planning and Development : Theory, Practice and Training,* Routledge, London.

Rosaldo and Lamphere, 1982, Signs, Vol. 8.

SAARC, *Guide Book on Women in Development.*

Santhanam, M.L. (1984), "Community Participation : A Case Study", *Social Change,* June, Vol.14.

Sood, Rita, 1991, *Changing Status and Adjustment of Women,* Manak Publications Pvt. Ltd. Delhi, First Edition.

8

WOMEN AND MEDIA: THE INDIAN SCENARIO

Dr.(Mrs.) Madhusmita Mishra

Women constitute about half of the population of any given society including that of India. So any study on social change and development must include the role, status and condition of women in the social system concerned. The women's issues include all those aspects that are related to their individual, group and social existence and well-being. These may range from provision of basic necessities of life for women by the society to that of steps taken by the state for improving their overall quality of life. Again, the issues like eradication of social apathy towards the problems of women, like various kinds of violence against women such as, female infanticide and dowry death also come to the picture in this context.

So far as the approaches to the study of Indian women are concerned, there exist two very important standpoints. One is the oriental or Indian approach that characterises Indian women as the symbol of sacrifice, purity, faithfulness, submission and devotion. On the other hand, there is the Western viewpoint, mostly found in English and American writings, which portrays the bulk of the Indian women as illiterate, backward and suppressed. But the fact remains somewhat in between. It is a reality that in comparison to men, Indian women are much less developed in terms of literacy, education and economic well being. But at the same time, the so-called illiterate and backward women, living in rural area, contribute substantially to the overall productive endeavours in the agricultural and allied sectors of the Indian economy. Again, after Independence, Indian women, primarily from the urban area, who have got reasonable opportunities for higher education, training and employment, have established their credentials in various walks of the socio-political life of India. Considering from the qualitative point of view, such women may be less in number, that quality-wise their achievement can hardly be over-emphasised.

Indian women, in spite of great hardships and societal hazards faced by them throughout the ages, have played a very significant role in social, cultural, economic and political spheres. It may be noted that women in India, one of the most ancient societies in the world, is known for a number of feminine virtues like compassion, tenderness, gentleness, courage of conviction and remarkable patience in the face of serious problematic situations.

Historically speaking, the status and position of women in ancient India are to be found in the classics and texts like the *Vedas*. The *Rigveda* contains that women enjoyed equal status with men regarding education in ancient India. Even some of the *Suktas* of the *Rigveda* were attributed to women seers who were known as "*rishikas*" and "*brahmavadinis*". Other Vedas also subscribe to this viewpoint. The position of women, during the middle ages deteriorated largely due to the impact of alien rule and foreign domination. The period from the invasion of India by Muhammad Ghori to that of the establishment of the British empire in the second half of the 18th century was the worst, so far as the condition of women in India was concerned. Even, until the emergence of social reform movements in the 19th century, there was no change in the status of women in India. Social reform movement along with the National Movement for Independence became the landmarks in the history of women's development in India. Attainment of independence and the adoption of the Constitution of India in 1950 marked the beginning of a new era in context to the equality, right and freedom for women in India. A number of social laws had been enacted to provide emancipation, welfare, development and empowerment of women. But surprisingly, all these provisions remain as only legal codes in the statute books and women's position has not been improved accordingly.

Despite the social legislation and planned development, women need to be educated and become aware of their rights, duties and responsibilities, so that, they will enjoy the benefits of development as well as they will have contributions for the progress of the nation and society. In this context, mass media have got important roles to play, that is, to project women in their proper role, status and identity as well as to inculcate the values, beliefs and orientations towards the polity and society in the minds of women and in the minds of citizens in general. Mass media contribute to the progress of the women and the society by articulating as well as aggregating the issues and problems of women to provide the input for making the public policies for women.

The main and special function of mass media is mass communication. Mass media transmit messages to a large number of audiences, irrespective of age, sex, and ethnicity within a short period of time. Communication does not exist in a vacuum. It is an integral part of our social, economic and cultural life. The communication process acts according to the prevailing social norms and takes the help of the media, which are available at any given point of time. For instance, mysticism, a method of communicating one's realisation and understanding of the God and His creation is an example of intra-personal communication. In this case, the medium is our faith or belief system. Many research findings point out that one of the primary focuses of interest in communication has been how does the receiver make sense of the stimuli or messages, that he or she receives so as to deepen his or her self-awareness.

In a sense, the Indian view of communication including its media takes into consideration the individual human being and his or her environment as integral parts of an interactive mechanism as against the quantitative and mechanical view of the West. The inventions and the use of technology have added new dimensions to the verbal and written words as tools of communication. The modern media like the press including the newspapers, magazines and books, and the audio-visual media like radio, television, video, internet computers and satellites have multiplied words and their interpretations which in turn have led to innumerable uses of the words.

India is no doubt, a stratified and hierarchical society. Throughout the ages, communication has tended to flow from the persons of higher status to those of lower status in the social hierarchy. Similarly, majorities of women were also at the receiving end of the communication system as the media of communication were mostly managed and manipulated by men. A number of factors in modern India including those of spread of English and liberal education, use of electricity and other scientific and technological innovations and the attainment of independence have revolutionised the situation. But the fact remains that despite passing from the first information and communication revolution, i.e., printing to the next such revolution, i.e., electronics and computers, the Indian society has also retained the traditional, oral and inter-personal communication side by side with other means of mass media. When we consider the characteristic features of the modern society, it is not the mass of people or their number that constitutes a mass society of the modern times, but it refers to the web of the inter-personal relationships that exist among the people. In this context, the role of mass media in the present-day India assumes a special significance. Such a large and heterogeneous society like the Indian social system requires a very effective communication system in which various media should work simultaneously to inform, educated and motivate the common people of the sub-continent.

So far as the question of portrayal of women in media is concerned, it may be printed out that the growing trend of depicting violence and vulgarism in the films and TV programmes has mostly targeted women who are at the receiving end. Several studies have found the audio-visual media guilty of sexism, distortion of the image of Indian women and propagation of sex stereotypes. Usually, most women are shown as playing a secondary and passive role in films and TV programmes.

Again the commercial advertisements, particularly in the TV, depict women in such a manner that cannot be termed as decent or civilised in any standard. In a number of cases, women or their images are used as objects and which are totally devoid of any context. Moreover, the bulk of the TV programmes and films highlight the upper class, urban and educated women and side-track the image of the average Indian woman belonging to the working class or the peasantry. For instance, in the TV programmes relating to agriculture, always the participants as well as the experts and specialists are males. Rarely, we have found women participating in such programmes either as farmers or as experts inspite of the fact that women contribute the most in that agricultural sector in India. It may be pointed out that the audio-visual media in India should try for the wholesome depiction of various categories of women such as educated and illiterate, urban and rural, or upper middle or lower class women. Indian women who belong to various socio-cultural backgrounds perform different types of work or profession and play multiple roles in their day to day life should be projected adequately in the media. Again, a few programmes that address woman and women's issues boil down to those urging them to adopt family planning measures or to be conscious of the need for pre-natal and post-natal care and similar themes.

So far as the portrayal of women in the print media is concerned, it may be pointed our that in a majority of cases, unfortunate events like dowry-deaths and torture, rape or eve-teasing incidents hit the headlines. As such, violence against women becomes news. But the real issues and problems of women such as illiteracy, economic exploitation, health hazards and inhuman service conditions of working women etc. are seldom given priority. A few women like Ms. Medha Patkar et. al. attract the attention of the media by virtue of their personal achievements. The situation has undergone some change after the advent of women reporters and journalists working in different media at various levels.

However, research findings point out that throughout the world, employment of women in the media is low, especially at decision-making levels in various media organisation. Men not only outnumber women in absolute terms but also constitute the majority of the management and high level editorial ranks in the media both in the developed and the developing countries. The Mac Bride Commission in its UNESCO-sponsored study has pointed out that journalists dealing with serious issues and political events are seldom women, and few women become editors or hold directing positions.

The Working Group on Software for Doordarshan, popularly known as the Joshi Committee in its report in 1985 pointed out the failure of our national endeavours to raise the status of women through the constitutional guarantees and developmental measures. It suggested that the portrayal of women in mass media should take note of all facets of women's lives in India today.

To conclude, we may point out that at present, there are a number of women writers, journalists, technical persons and computer professionals in the media. But only a handful of them like Nalini Singh, Mrinal Pandey or Arundhati Roy have made it to the top. So, Indian women will have to go a long way vis-à-vis the media.

REFERENCES

Agarwal, Binod C. and Kumkum Rai, 1988, *Women, Television and Rural Development*, New Delhi, National Publishing House.

Ahuja, B.N., 1988, *History of Press, Press Laws and Communications*, New Delhi, Surjeet Publications.

Bhattacharjee, Arun, 1972, *Indian Press: Profession to Industry*, New Delhi, Vikas Publications.

Editorial, 1997, New Form of Prasar Bharati , *The Dharitri*, (Oriya Daily), Bhubaneswar, November 2.

Editorial, 1997, Towards Autonomy , *The Times of India*, New Delhi, November 1.

Ghosh, Subir, 1991, *Mass Media Today: In The Indian Context*, Calcutta, Profile Publishers.

Joseph, Ammu and Kalpana Sharma (eds.), 1994, *Whose News; The Media and Women's Issues*, New Delhi, Sage Publications.

Joshi, P.C. *et al.*, 1985, *Report of the Working Group on Software for Doordarshan*, New Delhi.

Krishnan, Prabha and Anita Dighe, 1990, *Affirmation and Denial: Construction of Feminity on Indian Television*, New Delhi, Sage Publications.

MacBride, Sean, *et al.*, 1980, *Many Voices: One World*, Report by the International Commission for the Study of Communication Problems, Paris, UNESCO.

Mishra, Madhusmita, 1996, *Press and Political Socialisation*, (Unpublished Ph.D. Thesis), Bhubaneswar, Utkal University.

Verghese, B.G. *et al.*, 1978, *Report* of the National Broadcasting Trust—Akash Bharati, New Delhi, Vol. I and II.

9

COMMUNALISM AND WOMEN

Anil Dutta Mishra

The purpose of this paper is to analyse the issue involved in communalism and the way fundamentalism is increasing in India after Independence. Communalism is no more, only a political phenomenon. Directly or indirectly, it has entered in every aspect of Indian social life, posing a great threat to democracy, sovereignty and integration of the nation.

The following hypotheses are posited here for the purpose of critical discussion:

a) Communal organisations by raising women issues curtail women's fundamental rights.
b) By reinforcing religious traditions and fundamentalism, women's rights are curbed.
c) The communal tensions, riots and violence suppress women's survival, rights and freedom.
d) By raising the bogey of religion and communalism, it divides the women and weaker gender as a category and women's movement.

Communalism is perhaps one of the most intractable problems of the Indian polity and society, fast taking on an explosive form that threatens to blow up the very foundation of our national life. Communalism becomes a means to achieve the political goal. In fact, communalism has been a feature of Indian political culture throughout this century. Communalism directly or indirectly casts shadow on development of the society in general and women in particular. Communalism always curtails the women's rights and keeps them away from the mainstream. But, the introduction of women's issues in communalism is a recent phenomenon. The way, issues of women are coming in the grip of communalism, has drawn the attention of the social scientists.

Communalism becomes a means of exploitation, of furthering one's own objectives, of capturing power — political, religious, economic, social or otherwise, of perpetuating obscurantism and of projecting one's own image. Recent history has shown that every time there is a return to the so called fundamentalism of religion — any religion — there is, at the same time, a fundamentalist assault on women's freedom and identity. Through fundamentalism, women are twice victimised — first, on account of their gender and then, on account of religion. It is here that debate on communalism, fundamentalism and religious revivalism links up with the question of women's issues.

CONCEPT OF COMMUNALISM

To understand the communal phenomenon in India, one has to understand what is communalism and its implications in Indian society. Communalism is the manifestation of that philosophy which stands for the promotion of interests of a particular community based on religion, caste or language. Communalism is not just riots and social conflicts; it is something that has its roots in communal ideologies. Prof. Bipan Chandra[1] believes that communal ideology develops through three basic stages. First, it is the belief that people, who follow the same religion, have common secular interests, that is, common political, economic, social and cultural interests. This is the first bedrock of communal ideology. The second stage of communal ideology rests on the notion that in a multi-religious society like India, the secular interests, of the followers of one religion are dissimilar and divergent from the interests of the followers of another religion. The third stage of communalism is reached when the interests of the followers of different religions or of different communities are seen to be mutually incompatible, antagonistic and hostile. But, communal ideologies, being ideologies, must themselves have intellectual roots. Now, here the question arises: what are those roots? What is the precise form and content of the various communal ideologies in India? Why are they so popular in Indian social life? And how shall we intellectually triumph over them? These are the burning questions that one has to look into.

Leftist explanation of communalism is that communal forces are encouraged by the capitalists for their economic interests. Religion is also used as a tranquiliser. But, when they want to create disturbance, then also they take the help of religion. In this way, the Leftists have blamed the capitalists class for resorting to religious sentiments of people to secure their interest in all possible manners. On the other hand, Rightists' reaction to communalism is based on the theory of religious intolerance. In fact, communal question is not a simple one, it is highly complex phenomenon like any other social phenomenon. Worsening economic condition, increasing unemployment, frustration, a sense of social deprivation and a constant fear of loss of identity and status created an atmosphere of conflict, and paved the way for communalism to flourish. The electoral politics – nomination of the candidates, campaigning, communal representation etc. – accentuated the process of communalism in almost every state.

T.K. Ooman has suggested five dimensions of communalism, namely, assimilationist, welfareist, retaliatory, separatist and secessionist. Communalism can also be practiced in many ways like political communalism, religious communalism and economic communalism. Communalism in any form and colour assumes notoriety. It thrives whenever there is a difference between communities over religion, race, caste or language, or all of them. Communalism, which is sustained due to difference over religion is most powerful. The religious communalism is the most dominant amongst other forms of communalism.[2] Whatever it may be in popular parlance, whenever communalism is talked about, it refers to the religious communalism which is hinted at. Communalism has been understood in the above sense in this article.

WOMEN'S ISSUES AND COMMUNALISM

Women's issue is basically one that affects women directly or indirectly. In other words, any social evil perpetrated at the cost of women, any law or custom that reinforces and institutionalises women's inferior status in society, or any event or series of events that affects large number of women can be regarded as a woman's issue. Women's issues are also those that galvanise large numbers of women into action. Any such issues, which catch the attention of women's groups, and subsequently of the media, there are a myriad of other women's issues that are perennial, those that impinge on the life, health and work of women are women's issues.

The last few years have seen a concerted effort by the more militant religious organisations to revive obscurantist practices in the name of 'upholding traditions', and maintaining identity. Fundamentalist assault on women's freedom and identity are increasing from time to time. Threats have been perceived to the sanctity of religious customs, myths have been recreated and transformed 'identities' are daily being arbitrarily constructed and propagated as the trust representations of community. The phenomenon of restrictions passed by Punjab militants on women is a fundamentalism, but latter becomes communal because it demarcates Hindu and Sikh women, which can be used for political purposes.

Fundamentalism of any kind always curtails women's rights. For instance, Shah Bano case resulted in nation-wide campaign by the Muslim fundamentalists, which resulted in changing the Muslim Personal Law in favour of Fundamentalists. In Deorals (Rajasthan), a young widow was forced to burn herself alive to uphold the religious practices. Thousands of her pictures were displayed. A big Sati Mela (fair) was organised at that place in the name of protecting the customs. Some political leaders patronised this fair. In fact, this is not only a crime against women but against entire humanity.

In Punjab, the Bhindrawale Tiger Force of Khalistan, the Khalistan Commando Force, the Sikh Students Federation and Dashmesh Regiment of Khalistan had ordered women to give up western clothing, wear the *salwar-kameez* and veil their heads with the *dupatta*. The militants warned that a close watch would be kept on colleges and action would be taken, if women did not comply with the order within a fortnight. But, at the same time, there was no order banning western clothes for men. Another blow to women's status was the abortive attempt some years ago to draft a Sikh Personal Law, which denied women property rights.

The domain of Personal Laws is the most obvious and most fiercely contested of these sites. The first battle in the Babri Masjid – Ram Janambhoomi was, after all, won over the denial of rights to Muslim women in the Shah Bano controversy. The Mandir-Masjid dispute might well be fought to death on the streets of India, but few years ago, it was Muslim women who were the first to be sacrificed at the altar of an "identity" defined by religious customs. At last, one sacred institution that of Personal Laws—was forever secured by Muslim fundamentalists. For, it was women's rights that were being negotiated, their individual and gender identity naturally had to be subsumed in order to affirm community identity, and establish separateness from the majority.

For women, the coming together of religious fundamentalism and a partisan state, as seen in both the

Shah Bano and Roop Kanwar incidents, means the reconstitution of several patriarchies that they deal with every day of their lives. At home, the authority of the male is strengthened and under religious practice, women are systematically denied fundamental rights; their mobility and access to opportunity are circumscribed; they are further disabled by the imposition of an identity that militants against their identity as women. Christian women can not divorce their husband; Muslim women can not claim maintenance from them; Hindu women, who are part of the great Hindu undivided family can not be co-partner. Sikh women, had the Sikh Personal Law came into effect (as demanded by the fundamentalists) would not be entitled to inherit from their father, while Sikh widows would be required to marry their brothers-in-law, irrespective of the latter's age or marital status. In fact, fundamentalism is a curse for women's development. Even, in the communal violence women not only suffer as members of the attacked community, but they also suffer as women.

The simplistic explanation of this phenomenon may be that, women are half of the population and they constitute the largest section of practising believers. They are crucial to the economics of religious practices. Vested interests keep them ignorant and under subjection, thereby ensuring a dependable clientele. At another level, fundamentalism ties up with the women's question, because it is essentially a politically activated power game. Under the garb of protecting women and tradition, it exploits them in order to achieve its political and economic objectives. In fact, the real villain behind all the problems is the unbridled materialism that has taken charge of us. It is therefore, of little relevance what religious colour one wears, because fundamentalism is another banner for an entry into the power game. The electoral politics accentuate the process of communalism almost everywhere in India. It is here that, the debate on communalism and religious revivalism links up with the question of women's issues.

Recently, women have started participating in communal movement in a small way. In Jammu and Kashmir alone, large number of Muslim women, along with fundamentalists have campaigned for *burqa* (viel for women) under the banner of women's organisations like Al Fatima Liberation Force, Fanat-ul-Islam etc. On the other hand, Hindu women also participated in *Kar Seva* and received the *Rath* (chariot) of Advani at different places.

During recent riots in Bombay, women were also seen, pointing house of a particular community, which is a clear-cut indication of participation of women in communal riots. But at the same time, when we talk about the women's participation in communalism, one must have to clear on the nature and extent of their participation and why and under what circumstances they are participating.

One may conclude by saying that the real villain behind all the problems is power politics. The kind of politics that has been practised in India during the last two decades has greatly contributed to the strengthening of religious fundamentalism. It is therefore, of little relevance what religious colour one wears because fundamentalism is another banner for a quick entry into the power game. It is here that, the debate on communalism and religious revivalism links up with the question of women's issues in light of present political culture prevailing in India since Independence.

REFERENCES

1. Chandra, Bipan, (ed.), 1989, *India's Struggle for Independence*, Penguin, New Delhi, pp. 398-99.
2. Ahuja, Ram, 1992, *Social Problems in India*, Rawat Publications, Jaipur, p. 105.

10

KAMMA POLITICAL ELITE IN ANDHRA PRADESH AND WOMEN'S EQUAL RIGHT TO PROPERTY

H. Nageswara Rao

Equal right to property has been enshrined in the Constitution of India and several laws made thereunder have provided equal right to property to women. But in reality, women in Andhra Pradesh are still being deprived of this constitutional and legal right.

Women's demand for equal right to property with that of her husband, brother, father or son has now become vociferous and has taken the form of a movement in Andhra Pradesh. In the present study, an attempt is made to explain the relation of Kamma political elite with this movement. The present study is purely an empirical study based on the interviews with the Presidents of the Panchayat Samithis, because it was conducted at a time, when the 'Mandal system' was not introduced in the state.

However, the Kamma leaders under study are identified into four groups, namely, legislators, Panchayati Raj leaders, Ministers and party leaders. Their numbers and percentage are given in the following table.

TABLE - 1

Designation of Kamma Political Leaders

Sl.No.	*Designation*	*Numbers*	*Per cent*
1	Legislators	75	60.5
2	Panchayat Leaders	31	25.0
3	Ministers	12	9.7
4	Party Leaders	06	4.8
	TOTAL	124	100

Out of a total estimate of 150 Kamma political leaders, 124 respondents were interviewed. Special care has been taken to ensure that the political leaders of four different categories were included in the list of leaders. The above table shows that out of 124 leaders studied in this sample, 60.5% belonged to the 'Legislators" category consisting of Members of Legislative Assembly, Members of Legislative Council and Members of Parliament. This is the largest group. Care was also taken to ensure that the present legislators as well as ex-legislators were included in this category. As far as possible, the list included the elected representatives belonging to almost all political parties in the state. 'Panchayat Leaders' category consisted of Panchayat Samiti Presidents and Zilla Parishad Chairmen. They constituted 25% of this study. Specially, Samiti Presidents are included in this study because of the status and powers enjoyed by them. Practically they were equal to M.L.As. in all respects. Some of them wielded enormous influence in the rural areas, even to the extent of elected M.L.As. from the same area.

Mandal Presidents were nowhere near the Samiti Presidents in power and prestige. The inclusion of this category of respondents in this study provided valuable information and data about the socio-economic background and perceptions; and political background as well as the relevant perceptions of this category of political leaders. In this very category, Kamma Zilla Parishad Chairmen were also studied. The status and importance of Zilla Parishad Chairman is well known. Their position is equivalent to that of the Ministers at the state level. Practically, they are the sole monarchs of their concerned district, very much to the envy of even Cabinet Ministers. At the top of their popularity and necessary support from the state government forthcoming in abundance, the entire district administration was at their feet. The present Zilla Parishad Chairman as well ex-Chairman were included in the sample of this study, whereas in the case of Panchayat Samiti Presidents only the present incumbents were included in this study. Ministers, who constituted third category of Kamma political leaders, formed 9.7% of the sample studied. The list included the present and the past incumbents, who held the post. Many respondents, who were interviewed as M.L.As later, became Ministers in the Cabinet reshuffles that took place later on from time to time. Since their promotion from M.L.A. to Minister post came after their interview was held, they were kept in the category of M.L.As only. In order to make the study complete and all comprehensive, leaders holding important party posts, such as 'President' and 'Secretary' (present and past) were also studied in the fourth category of 'Party Leaders". This category constituted 4.8% of leaders. Every attempt is made to make this study well-rounded and comprehensive analysis of the Kamma political elite in Andhra Pradesh.

TABLE - 2

Kamma Leaders' Support for Women's Equal Right to Property

Sl. No.	*Response*	*Numbers*	*Per cent*
1	Yes	107	86.3
2	No	17	13.7
Total		124	100.00

Data in the above table deals with the Kamma Political Leaders' support for or opposition to Women's Equal Right to property. While 86.3 per cent of Leaders supported, 13.7 per cent of them opposed equal right to property to women. It is interesting to note that an overwhelming majority of the total sample studied gave their support to the cause of equal right to property to women.

TABLE - 3

Reasons for Supporting Women's Equal Right to Property

Sl.No.	*Reasons*	*Nos.*	*Per cent*
1	N.A.	17	13.7
2	Equality of sex	13	10.5
3	Economic Security to Women	5	4.0
4	Increases self-confidence	1	0.8
5	To abolish dowry	1	0.8
6	Economic uplift of family	19	15.3
7	To fight with social evils	68	54.8
	Total	124	100.00

Data in Table 3 deals with the reasons for support as given by the Kamma Political Leaders on Women's Equal Right to Property. 13.7 per cent of leaders belonged to 'Not Applicable' category, because they were opposed to women's equal right to property. While, 10.5 per cent leaders mentioned 'Equality of Sex' reasons for women's equal right to property, 4 per cent 'Economic Security to Women', 0.8 per cent for increasing the self- confidence among women, 0.8 per cent for abolishing dowry and 15.3 per cent gave reason that women having equal right to property could bring economic uplift of the family. However, majority of the respondents *(54.8%)* opined that by conferring equal right to property to women, women would be self-assertive and could fight with many social evils like dowry etc.

To sum up. The demand for women's equal right to property has not yet been obtained full support from the

Kamma leaders in Andhra Pradesh. It is doubtful that the movement for women's equal right to property will be successful when leaders are opposing it. Male chauvinism and conservatism are still present in the Society of Andhra Pradesh, for which, women fail to enjoy social equality and economic security, even if the Constitution and several social laws guarantee equal right to property to women.

11

WOMEN AND THEIR WORK ENVIRONMENT

Dr.(Mrs.) Swarnamayee Tripathy

Participation in economic and political field is crucial to women's struggle for a better social status. The advent of industrialisation in India during the British rule, the introduction of western education, the intrusion of modern values into the Indian society had brought significant changes in the lives of women. The process of developmental changes has been accelerated by the Constitution of Independent India, which granted gender equality with the aim to establish equalitarian democratic society. In present days, more and more women are visible in politics and in white-collar as well as blue-collar occupations and millions are seeking employment. Once declared as a spent force, these women have seen the elevation of their status in social, economic, personal and legal spheres.

Moreover, working together in groups in the production process has given women a better exposure to public affairs and created group feeling among women. Objective work condition creates awareness among women. A secured job, a good salary along with perks and benefits, a considerate employer help in encouraging the participation of workers in union activities. Subjective awareness of one's own social position and of one's exploitation may inspire her to realise the necessity of sharing political power. Trade unionism is a step in this direction.

However, social and economic condition of women workers indicates that the women workers do not constitute a truly homogeneous social class. The internal differences are further heightened by even more pronounced differences in the work environment of these workers.

The present study is an attempt to examine the work environment of the women workers and their subjective perception of the objective work conditions. The term 'worker' as defined in Factories Act, 1948 refers to a person employed directly or through any agency in any manufacturing process. It excludes persons holding positions of supervision and management.[1] In other words, it includes all manufacturing units in public and private sector, which are regulated by the State through its Industrial Acts.

Again the term 'work-environment' can be defined in a variety of ways because of its multi-dimensionality. A survey carried out in the United States used the term working conditions as mainly comprised of wages, fringe benefits, health and safety, travel to and from work, steady employment, recruitment relationship with supervisor and fellow workers and future prospects at work.[2] In the present study, we have taken those aspects of work conditions, which bear a deep impact on the personality of the workers.

The present study has selected three Industrial Estates in Orissa for observation and analysis. It has been assumed that in-group interaction among these industrial population having identical problems may create group consciousness within them. Further, they being nearer to the townships easily avail the modern amenities. If we see these industrial estates as sub-systems within a larger social system, the sub-system can not escape interactions with the surrounding social and political system.

This research work is based on a sample selected from women employed in the industries in three industrial areas, namely, Madhupatna, Choudwar and Jagatpur in the district of Cuttack in Orissa, a State of the Indian Union. This sample selection is based on the consideration that the district of Cuttack has a long history of industrial growth. Cuttack is a coastal district in eastern Orissa having highest population (17.57%) of the total population of the State and is more exposed to urban life.[3] Out of 91,319 women workers in the district are 34,531, who are employed in public and private undertakings.[4] Cuttack has three industrial growth centres namely, Madhupatna, Choudwar and Jagatpur that had been developed to reduce the burden on the largest city of Orissa, i. e., the Cuttack city. It has been observed that these growth centres provide the workers with a community life.

Field studies have been conducted through the use of survey method based on personal observation and interview. Respondents were interviewed on the basis of both structured and open-ended questions. Interviewing was supplemented by systematic and non-participant observation facilitated by frequent visits to the factories. For example, relationships between employer and employees and on trade union participation of respondents we had to depend to a large extent on our observation. Since the official register of industries does not include the name of casual workers and these workers are hired by local contractors attached to the respective industries, it is difficult to know the exact number of women in these industries. Therefore, through random sampling 152 women workers were taken for analysis.

The present study is divided into four sections. Section I gives a brief information of female work participation rate in the country. Section II analyses working condition of the women workers. Section III makes a study of awareness of the respondents. Section IV deals with the objective consciousness of their socio-economic exploitation on the part of women workers.

WOMEN IN LABOUR MARKET

Employment of women in gainful activities has been considered as the critical entry point to country's development. Increasing educational opportunities for women in post-independent India and technological advancement have created a number of job opportunities for women. As a result, women's participation in the work force of the country has increased numerically, though the rate of increase has been marginal. The total female working population accounts for 100 million in the year 1988 and 2 million more women are added to female labour force every year.[5] It has been observed that a large number of women are engaged in agricultural activities either as cultivators or agricultural labourers. With growing industrialisation the share of women in the organised sector has increased from 8 per cent in 1981 to 13.03 per cent in 1988.[6] In household industries, out of every 100 persons, 36.5 are ladies. Also, women constitute 5.8 per cent of the All-India Services. Their participation in service sector as doctors, nurses, teachers is relatively increasing. Thus, though marginal, there has been an increase in employment of women in all sectors.

However, a small section of women have entered into the work-force inspite of the efforts of Government and different voluntary agencies. In 1991, 22.73 per cent of women in the country are engaged in some kinds of economic activities.[7] In Orissa, less than one-fifth of the female population has employment and one-tenth of them are engaged in many economic activities. Also, female work participation rate is proportionately larger in the unorganised sector of the economy. This reveals the pressure on women to take up any employment offer whatever the arduousness and whatever the way. That is why female work participation rate among the poor or lower middle class is positively higher in number.

Despite the changing socio-economic environment in

India, sex inequality still continues to exist in different levels of society and women's position is still subjugated and dependent. Some micro studies reveal that the job market in India has developed a sex dimension. 'Femininity' and 'masculinity' have been gradually attached to different jobs which ultimately brings lower wages to women. In agriculture, works that fetch higher wages like ploughing are 'male' preserves and ones like transplanting in which women are of higher proportion of work force bring lower wages to women. Women are concentrated in few industries like readymade garments, embroidery and electronic industries.

WOMEN WORKERS AND THEIR WORK ENVIRONMENT

Social deprivation, economic subjugation and dependence of Indian women manifest in exploitation at three different levels, namely, at the family level, in work place and also at political level by the political parties, pressure groups and trade unions. The patriarchal values and attitudes of our stratified society have placed women in a secondary position in the family. This has affected women's development in the fields of education, employment, health and public activity. Even the educated and professionally qualified women in India find it difficult to escape the disadvantages of their womanhood.

Wages, benefits and job-security have been taken as reliable indicators of the working conditions. On this basis, it has been found in our study that women work in deplorable working conditions. The working conditions of the respondents of our sample are far from satisfactory. The socio-economic profile of the respondents reveals that the labour market is not neutral to men and women. Since a majority of women workers lack any technical knowledge or proper education, technological advancement had forced them to opt for unskilled and semi-skilled jobs with low wages.

WAGES

Our findings on wages show that a large percentage of women workers of our sample received very low wages. They receive less than the average wage of Rs.439.00 per month. The wage structure of the sample (Table 1) of women workers indicates that 5 per cent of the sample received a salary more than Rs.900/-, but less than Rs. 1000/-. It is significant to note that 68 per cent of our respondents have either no or little education, and usually earn Rs.150/- or Rs.200/- per month in the beginning of their employment. That salary reaches the level of Rs.350/- per month after seven or eight years of service.[8] Lack of education does not create any facility for technical education, high salary or steady employment. As a result, women workers have added to the reserve army of unskilled workers.

TABLE – 1

Wage Structure of Respondents

(N= 152)

Education/ Wage Income (per month)	*Illi-terate*	*Primary*	*High school*	*College*	*Total*	*% of total*
Below Rs.300/-	38	10	02	00	50	32.89
Below Rs.500/-	32	04	10	02	48	31.58
Below Rs.700/-	10	02	20	04	36	23.68
Below Rs.900/	—	06	04	—	10	6.58
Rs.900/- and above	—	—	04	04	08	4.26
Total	80	22	40	10	152	100.00

JOB SECURITY AND BENEFITS

Job security is affected by the terms of employment conditions in the factory. If the job security is less, the benefits accruing to workers become less. In the present study, a cross table of the nature of job security and the benefits through wages is given below.

TABLE – 2

Job Security of Respondents

(N= 152)

Income/ Nature of Job	*Below Rs. 300/-*	*Below Rs. 500/-*	*Below Rs. 700/-*	*Below Rs. 900/-*	*Rs. 900/- and above*	*Total*	*Per cent*
Daily Wage	—	—	18	—	—	18	11.84
Casual	44	26	04	—	—	74	48.68
Part-time	06	—	—	—	—	06	03.94
Permanent	—	22	14	10	08	54	35.53
Total	50	48	36	10	08	132	100.00

The temporary and casual nature of the jobs of majority (65 per cent) of women workers did not bring them high salary or any facility at the work place. From the table given above, it is found that 33% of women workers whose salary is less than Rs.300/- per month are either casual or part time workers. Only 35.53% of women workers in our sample receive a monthly salary on a regular basis. Thus, because most of the women workers are engaged as casual and part-time workers. They are low paid. So, the employment condition does not favour them to earn better livelihood.

Likewise, women generally do not get any tangible benefits like casual leave. Earned leave, medical or maternity leave. In theory, they are always entitled to these benefits but seldom get them in reality. The permanent of job status of some respondents has been achieved due to their longer period of service to the industry, but it does not accrue them facilities, like provident fund, gratuity etc. that are associated with permanent status of any government jobs. Further the question of giving the benefits to temporary or casual workers do not arise at all.

If wages, benefits and job security are taken as reliable indicators of the working conditions, then there is no doubt that most of the women workers are working in a 'work-environment', which is not favourable to them.

JOB SATISFACTION AND COMMITMENT

Extent of job-commitment is a sufficient indication of the fact that the respondent is satisfied with her work-environment. This will gradually result in intense interaction with the other members of the industrial system and involvement in the affairs of the industry. This can be studied from the following view-points.

1. Attitude towards present job
2. Desire to pursue the occupational career

A working woman has dual responsibilities to dispense with – one is the duty in the family and the other is activities at work place. In most cases, the jobs to which women workers have access involve routine, monotonous and low-paid work with little or no future prospects. Therefore, the working class women workers in low-paid jobs having a temporary status may not develop a strong attachment to their job. It has been observed that 65% of our sample earn less than their average wage of Rs.439/- per month. 64 per cent of these are either casual labourers or daily-wage worker or part-time workers. (Table – 2). 83% of our sample are engaged in some kind of manual work. Being in such conditions, most of our respondents are quite ambivalent to their present jobs. This is evident in Table – 3.

This table shows that only very marginal respondents (11.84%) are satisfied with their job. Those respondents, who are not satisfied with their jobs, belong to lower income group.

TABLE – 3

Respondent's Reaction to their Present Jobs by Income Variation

(N= 152)

Income/ Response	*Below Rs. 300/-*	*Below Rs. 500/-*	*Below Rs. 700/-*	*Below Rs. 900/-*	*More than Rs. 900/-*	*Total*	*Per cent*
Daily Wage	—	—	18	—	—	18	11.84
Satisfied	08	-02	02		06	18	11.84
Somewhat Satisfied	02	36	24	08	02	72	47.36
Not Satisfied	40	12	10	—	—	62	40.80
Total	50	48	36	10	08	152	100.00

TABLE – 4

Change for Better Jobs desired by Respondents (Income Variation)

(N= 152)

Income/ Desire to Change the Job	*Below Rs. 300/-*	*Below Rs. 500/-*	*Below Rs. 700/-*	*Below Rs. 900/-*	*More than Rs. 900/-*	*Total*	*Per cent*
Yes	50	40	34	10	06	148	97.37
No	—	—	02	—	02	04	2.63
Total	50	40	36	10	08	152	100.00

This table indicates that 97.37% of the respondents are willing to change the job. Here income-variation does not count much. Respondents of all income groups want to change the job, as they are not satisfied with the work conditions. Even two-thirds of the respondents, who are getting more than Rs. 900/- want to change the present job.

TABLE – 5

Desire to Pursue the Professional Career by Caste Variation

Caste/ Career	*General*	*Schedule Caste*	*Schedule Tribe*	*Total*	*Per cent*
Wish to Continue Career	48	04	—	52	34.12
Don't wish to Continue Career	54	18	28	100	65.88
Total	102	22	28	152	100.00

The desire to pursue the occupational career creates keenness among the workers to change the work environment to suit their needs. Table 5 indicates that 66 of our respondents do not show any interest to pursue their career, if their financial condition would improve. Another sufficient indication of

TABLE – 6

Reasons for the Respondent's Taking Up Their Present Job

(N= 152)

Income / *Response*	*Below Rs. 300/-*	*Below Rs. 500/-*	*Below Rs. 700/-*	*Below Rs. 900/-*	*More than Rs. 900/-*	*Total*	*Per cent*
Economic Necessity	50	94	36	10	06	146	96.0 5
To Utilise Potential Capacity	—	02	04	04	02	12	7.9
Husband's negligence	10	04	—	—	—	14	9.21
To Increase Social Presitge	—	—	02	—	02	04	2.63
To Utilise Spare Time	—	—	02	02	—	04	2.63

their attitude is the unwillingness on the part of the working mother not to make her daughter lead a working life. Their commitment to career is mainly born out of economic necessity, that is, a characteristic of the working class families, who wish to achieve a better status. However, caste is not a factor to determine the choice of pursuing or not pursuing a career for women.

The above table points out that most of our respondents have stressed on economic necessity as the cause behind their taking up any job. It has also been noted that respondents having technical knowledge do not wish to discontinue with her career. Also, women workers having a better income do not want to give up their jobs. Our findings have distinctly differed from Kala Rani's and D'Souza's findings. They found that most of the women workers, whom they studied, came to work either to utilise their knowledge or to utilise their leisure. Apparently, this difference has to be attributed to the difference in the class status of the women workers. Our respondents have mostly come from low-economic working class background, whereas, samples in D'Souza's and Kala Rani's studies were drawn either from middle class or from the upper middle class women workers. Therefore, the difference can be seen in the light of difference in economic class.

However, the disinterest that shown in pursuing the occupational career is due to the low wages, deplorable working conditions and dual burden of both home and office bore by the women workers. "If I have money, I would give up working", is a wishful thinking for a female worker, who belong to poor working-class families. This information, we have gathered in course of our casual talk and discussion with the respondents during the interview. Our respondents being in their own environment are interested to continue working despite their dissatisfaction with the present jobs and the deplorable working condition.

AWARENESS OF EXPLOITATION

It is found from observation that the working conditions of women workers, objectively speaking, are quite bad in terms of wages, benefits and job security. This phenomenon of exploitation in an industrial society can hardly be disputed. In this context, several questions were asked to the respondents. Do the women workers have the awareness of their exploitation by their management or employers? Do they have any awareness of the problems at the work place? Do they have knowledge regarding legal rights and do they enjoy it? Do they complain before the employer for any problem at the work place? Do they perceive any enhancement of social status in the family, neighbourhood and among their relatives due to their economic independence? Undoubtedly, awareness of these issues will make the women workers conscious of the phenomenon of exploitation.

Generally, women workers have to bear a double burden both at home and work place. Their long absence from home creates certain problems for them. Over and above it, negative conditions of work like lack of guarantee of work, absence of some benefits like regular payment, maternity benefits, low wages have torn the women workers into pieces. Sometimes, they receive less wages than that of male workers. Even, in some industries, the workers have to face health hazards. They remain simply as objects of production. Being in such conditions, they loose the strength to change the environment to suit their psychological and physiological needs. The data presented in Table – 7 indicates that 89.47 % of respondents of our total sample consider heavy work- load as one of the problem of women workers. 80% of the sample could understand that, employers give irregular payment to the women workers. 77% of them perceive lack of guarantee of work as one of the most important problems, which threaten the psychology of workers. Half of the respondents complain that they get wage less than what the male workers get. Even, 37% of the respondents complain that they do not get maternity benefit. However, few respondents are quite aware of health hazards due to their routine work in factories.

TABLE – 7

Awareness of Respondents Regarding Problems At Work Place

N=152

Sl.No.	*Problems*	*No. of women workers*	*Per cent*
1	Heavy Workload	136	89.47
2	Unequal Payment	82	53.96
3	Irregular Payment	122	77.63
4	Lack of Guarantee of Work	118	77.63
5	Health Problem	12	7.92
6	Absence at home	52	34.20
7	Absence of maternity Benefit	56	36.84

Though, the women workers perceive their problems existing in their work environment, they are hardly aware of their rights. Our Constitution gives legal equality to both men and women. Government of India has given maternity benefits to women workers by the Maternity Benefit Act. It has also given to all workers the right to strike by Industrial Disputes Act in case of any justice done to them by the employer. Minimum Wages Act gives the right to women to get equal wages with men for similar work. Besides, the Government has compelled the employer to set up crutch near the industry, which has employed more than thirty women to look after their kids.

Legal awareness of our respondent has been measured in a 5-point scale. One point is given for being aware of one right. Respondent securing no points or 1 point has been categorised into a group having 'low' awareness. Respondents securing 2 or 3 points are considered as having 'medium' awareness, and more than that of having 'high' awareness. Thus, respondents have been categorised into three categories, namely, 'low', 'medium' and 'high' in terms of their level of

TABLE – 8

Legal Awareness of Respondents (Education-wise)

N=152

Education/ Legal Awareness	*Illiterate*	*Primary*	*High School*	*College*	*Total*	*Per cent*
Low	22	04	—	—	26	17.11
Medium	58	18	18	04	98	64.47
High	—	—	22	06	28	18.42

TABLE – 9

Legal Awareness of Respondents (Income-wise)

(N= 152)

Income *Awareness*	*Below Rs. 300/-*	*Below Rs. 500/-*	*Below Rs. 700/-*	*Below Rs. 900/-*	*More than Rs. 900/-*	*Total*	*Per cent*
Low	08	12	04	—	02	26	17.11
Medium	42	36	18	02	—	98	64.47
High	—	—	14	08	06	28	18.42
Total	50	48	36	10	08	152	100.00

legal awareness. It has been observed that women workers belonging to all income categories are conscious of their right to get equal wages for equal work and to get maternity leave. Contrary to it, very few are aware of the fact of constitutional equality of men and women. Almost all have no knowledge of right to have creche near the industry. Table – 8 shows that 64.47% of the total sample have medium level of awareness of legal rights. In other words, these women are aware of the right of equal wages and right to maternity benefit. Those women workers, who constitute only 17 per cent of the total sample, have no knowledge or little knowledge of legal rights and are mostly illiterate. It is also observed that respondents having matriculation or more qualification have 'medium' or 'high' level awareness. Table IX has also observed that women engaged in low-paid jobs have either low or medium level awareness. Thus, it can be concluded that education and income have positive correlation with level of legal awareness of respondents. However, women workers have minimum level of awareness of problems at the work place and of legal rights irrespective of level of income and education. After that, it seems to be increasing with the increase in the level of both education and income. The knowledge will help in creating political awareness or influencing participation in Union activities, but is not the sole determining factor. General apathy of these workers is responsible for their passivity.

After observing the perception of problems of the 'work-environment' and level of legal awareness, we have tried to observe the reaction of women workers to these problems.

TABLE – 10

Respondent's Reaction towards the Employers (Education-wise)

(N=152)

Do you complain?	*Illiterate*	*Primary*	*High School*	*College*	*Total*	*Per cent*
Yes	78	20	36	06	140	92.2
No	02	02	04	04	12	7.8
Total	80	22	40	10	152	100.00

The above table shows that 92% of the total sample respondents whether literate or illiterate complain before the employer about their inconveniences. It seems neither education nor income has any proportional influence on this activity of the workers.

In order to confirm this response, the respondents were asked another question: "do they consider union activities as useful?" In response to this question, 68.42 per cent of the sample did not answer at all, and only 27.63% of them answer in positive. They have high school or more educational qualification. Hence, those who have high educational qualification and legal awareness could understand the utility of collective action. Further, when union activity has been correlated with salary, it has been observed that a secured job and a comparatively high salary inspire the respondents to take interest in union activity. It has also been observed that since women workers are mostly engaged in low-paid jobs due to lack of technical knowledge, almost all of them are neither member of any trade union or conscious of the working of such unions in industries.

TABLE – 11

Respondent's Response to the Usefulness of Unionism (Education-wise)

N=152

Do you think that Union activities are useful?	*Illiterate*	*Primary*	*High School*	*College*	*Total*	*Per cent*
Yes	08	08	16	10	42	27.63
No	04	—	02	—	06	3.95
Do not know	68	14	22	—	104	68.42
Total	60	22	40	10	152	100.00

Majority of studies on women has been concluded that educational qualification and economic independence of women result in enhancement of their social status. By taking this assumption into consideration, our respondents were asked, whether they perceive any change in their social status. Different weights are attached to different responses, i.e., 'great extent', 'less extent', 'not at all', 'do not know'. Our main aim is to know how far do the women worker's perception of their own class-status match with their objective condition. It has been observed in the following two tables.

TABLE – 12

Perception of Social Status (Income-wise)

(N= 152)

Income / Response	*Below Rs. 300/-*	*Below Rs. 500/-*	*Below Rs. 700/-*	*Below Rs. 900/-*	*More than Rs. 900/-*	*Total*	*Per cent*
Great extent	—	—	04	—-	08	12	20.5
Less extent	02	04	—	02	—	08	10.25
Not at all	—	10	20	—	—	30	25.6
Do not know	48	34	12	08	—	102	43.59

TABLE – 13

Perception of Social Status (Education-wise)

N=152

Education/ Social Status	*Illiterate*	*Primary*	*High School*	*College*	*Total*	*Per cent*
Great Extent	02	00	04	06	12	20.5
Less Extent	00	02	06	00	08	10.25
Not at all	06	08	16	00	30	25.64
Do not know	72	12	07	04	102	43.59

The above two tables point out that 43.59% of the total sample do not have any subjective perception of the attitude of social environment towards them. 25.64% of the respondents feel that economic independence has not brought any change in their status either in the family or in the community. 20.5% of the sample respondents having education and a relatively higher monthly salary see some changes in their social status. Thus, it can be concluded that income, education and social status have significant relations.

CONCLUSION

It is found from our study that women workers are mostly engaged in low-paid jobs due to lake of education and technical knowledge. Negative conditions at the work-place have put more psychological pressure on women. Consequently, they remain simply as objects of production unable to change the environment to suit their psychological and physiological needs.

A majority of women workers are hardly aware of their legal rights except certain common rights like right to maternity benefits and right to equal payment. Their awareness of problems and prospects in the immediate environment is directly proportional to their level of education and income.

However, despite their awareness, women workers are not conscious of their exploitation by the industrial system. Had it been so, they would have had the consciousness of utility of collective bargaining. General apathy of these workers is responsible for their passivity.

Again, women workers do not have any perception of the attitude of social environment towards them. Perhaps, due to their little income, women workers are not able to bring any substantial change in their standard of living.

Thus, better educational and employment opportunities are fundamental to any improvement in the socio-economic conditions or status of women. There is an urgent need to uncover hidden social discrimination like attitudinal behaviour against women employment in India. Until work becomes women's right, they will continue to be discriminated. Ultimately, the only effective way to expand the small space, which the existing structure of society continue to confine them in, is for women to organise themselves to overcome their mental and material state of helplessness. Women's right to organise and struggle against their oppression must be linked with the question of democratic rights of the people.

REFERENCES

1. G.P.Sinha & P.R.N.Sinha, *Industrial Relations and Labour Legislation.*
2. University of Michigan Survey Research Center, 1976, *Survey of Working Conditions,* University of Michigan, Ann Arbor, U.S.A.
3. Government of India, *Census of India,* 1981
4. *Ibid.*
5. Statistics Presented at NGO Consultation on "Equality, Development, Peace", 1988, New Delhi.
6. *Ibid.*
7. India 1991 Census General Economic Tables
8. This has been found in the process of personal conversation with the respondents during interview.
9. Kala Rani, 1976, Role Conflict in Working Women, New Delhi, Chetana Publishers and also, V.D'Souza, (ed.), 1975, *Women in Contemporary India,* Manohar Prakashan, New Delhi.

12

WORKING WOMEN AND THEIR POLITICAL SOCIALISATION

Dr.(Mrs.) Sharada Rath
Ms. Gayatri Kar

Women constitute nearly half of the population of India. Now-a-days, women get better status because of education and employment. The change in the behavioural pattern and their status in the society have occurred in relation to their enhanced socio-economic conditions. Social justice strongly corresponds to equal participation of females in the production process of a nation. Thus, social justice demands that females must play an important and active role in the development of a nation or the society. Political involvement and participation of women in politics, nevertheless, would bring self-esteem and identity to women, as well as would help the building of the nation.

Working in the production process has given women a better exposure in public affairs and created group feeling among them. This has made them a class in itself and has brought political awareness, which is the basic necessity in a democratic system. But, if they get an employment, and being not conscious of their rights, do not participate in the decision-making process, they would be considered in their organisations, polity and society as second class citizens.

SCOPE AND OBJECTIVES

Along with economic emancipation, women's participation in the political process is an affirmation of social justice, human rights and egalitarianism in the society, as well as it gives due recognition to the potentialities of women's capability and contribution for the development and nation-building. But, political participation depends to a large extent upon the political awareness of the individual. Political awareness, values and orientations are created through a process of learning, which is otherwise known as socialisation process. Therefore, the main point of this article is to find out to what extent the working women are being socialised in order to develop a political self through awareness, interest and participation. The nature, extent and agents of socialisation of working women constitute the core areas of the present study. However, in order to arrive at a scientific conclusion, political socialisation study can be made by adopting an empirical method of inquiring the problem through field survey.

UNITS OF ANALYSIS

The units of analysis of the present study are the working women, who are employed in formal sectors of different kinds of jobs. The geographical scope of the present study is the Cuttack city (Orissa), where the samples of working women are chosen as units of analysis. We have distributed 100 schedules for eliciting responses, but we received only 60 schedules with complete answer to all the questions in the schedule. The response group consists of only working women of different age groups, of different educational qualifications, of different income level and of different occupations. These variables are taken as independent to explain the dependent variable, that is, the political socialisation. The following table indicates the socio-economic profile of the respondents.

TABLE – 1

Socio-economic Profile of the Respondents

N=60

Variables	*Components*	*Frequency*	*Percentage*
Age	21-30	07	11.66
	31-40	10	16.66
	41-50	24	40.00
	51 and above	19	31.66
Education	High School	09	15.0
	College	17	28.33
	University/Technical	34	56.66
Occupation	Teacher	14	23.33
	Lecturer	20	33.33
	Doctor	06	10.0
	Executive	04	6.66
	Administrator	05	8.33
	Clerks	11	18.33
Income(Monthly)	Below Rs.1500/-	08	13.33
	1501-2500	14	23.33
	2501-3500	18	30.0
	3501 and above	20	33.33
Marital Status	Married	35	58.33
	Unmarried	20	33.33
	Divorcee	05	8.33

POLITICAL SOCIALISATION: THE CONCEPT

Political socialisation is the process by which an individual becomes acquainted with the political system, which determines his/her perceptions of politics and his/her reactions to political phenomena. It refers to the process by which individuals learn the political norms, values and behaviour patterns of the nations, groups, or sub-groups to which they belong. It is concerned with how individuals acquire political cognition, attitudes, and behaviour. Political cognition refers to beliefs about the political system and knowledge of its institutions, officials and functioning. Political attitudes are positive or negative feelings, which one has toward the political system, public officials, political issues, and the political process itself. Political behaviour refers to the political involvement and political action, as well as evaluation of political phenomena.

Hyman (1959) laid emphasis on the perpetuation of political values across generations, through the learning process through which norms and behaviour patterns acceptable to the political system are being transmitted. Almond and Powell (1966) define political socialisation as a process through which an individual is inducted into political culture. It is the process through which political cultures are shaped, maintained and changed. Political socialisation thus helps an individual in the development of his awareness, interest and involvement in politics and thereby it creates a political self-identity. It makes the individual politically active to participate in the decision-making process. This also helps the system to persist as a democratic one, as people would develop their allegiance and obligation for the system because of their values, norms and behaviour, which have been inducted to them through the process of political socialisation.

Political socialisation is a never-ending process. It begins with the childhood stage of human being and it continues to the end of life. Therefore, Aristotle had rightly said, "Man is a political animal". Childhood learning has got lasting impression on the political orientation of individual. Political orientation at the adult stage has more or less been influenced by childhood learning. Sometimes, childhood orientation continues to be imprinted more and more, sometimes, it becomes totally changed, and it becomes more reformed and refined at the childhood stage. But, nevertheless, childhood learning has got much impact upon the political learning of the adulthood period. Therefore, the first question was asked to the sample respondents: "Would you please recollect and say at what stage you first come to hear/know about the political phenomena, like, about your country, its flag, national anthem, or President, Prime Minister, etc.?

TABLE – 2

Distribution of Respondents over the Question of Time of First Political Socialisation

(N=60)

Period of First Socialisation	*Number of Respondents*	*Per cent*
Below 6 years	05	8.33
6 to 16 years	17	28.33
17 to 22 years	30	50.0
23 years and above	08	13.33

The above table indicates that childhood socialisation of working women is not significant and most of the working women (50%) are being socialised after their school level education being completed. Adulthood socialisation through schools and colleges become more significant.

Only 8.33 per cent of sample women respondents have childhood socialisation. Their parents have university education. It is found that specially when the mothers are highly educated, women obtain their early socialisation. But, when the father is well educated and mother is not, early socialisation becomes impaired. In this study, it is found that the mothers who have university education, their girl-child invariably gets early socialisation. But, in the case of father's education, it is found that while fathers of 30 per cent of women respondents are highly educated, only 8.33% of their daughters have early socialisation. Therefore, early socialisation depends upon the education of the parents and specifically, upon the education of the mothers.

In order to find out the extent of socialisation of working women, a number of questions were put to the sample respondents. To know the names of the political persons constitutes one of the components of political knowledge of the individual. So the question was asked to name the persons like (a) the President of India, (b) The Prime Minister of India, (c) The Chief Minister of Orissa, (d) Local Member of the Legislative Assembly. One point was awarded for the correct answer of each question. The pattern of the extent of knowledge about political personalities has been given in the following table.

TABLE – 3

Distribution of Respondents over the Question of Knowledge of Political Personalities

N=60

Political	*To a great extent (4 points)*	*To some extent (3 points)*	*To less extent (2 points)*	*Not at all (1 Point)*
The President of India	27 (45%)	15 (25%)	13 (21.66%)	05 (8.33%)
The Prime- Minister of India	33 (55%)	17 (28.33%)	08 (13.33%)	02 (3.33%)
The Chief Minister of Orissa	42 (70%)	08 (13.33%)	10 (16.66%)	00
Local M.L.A.	15 (25%)	06 (10%)	12 (20%)	27 (45%)
Total	117 (48.75%)	46 (19.16%)	43 (17.91%)	34 (14.16%)

From the above table, it is found that in general 48.75% of the sample-working women know to a great extent the names of political personalities. But, to a lesser extent, they have the knowledge of the name of the local M.L.A., while to a greater extent, they know the name of the President of India, the Prime Minister and the Chief Minister of the State.

The existence and working of political parties in a democracy is a vital phenomenon. Partyless democracy is a political myth. Hence, the knowledge of the names of political parties at least indicates the extent of socialisation of the individual. Therefore, in this study, he names of certain parties were given and the respondent was asked to name the political parties, which she had heard of. If one knows more than five political parties, she has been given the award of "to a great extent", if between 3 to 5 political parties, "to some extent", if between 1 to 2 political parties, "to less extent". If one does not know the name of any political party, she has been given the award of "not at all". The picture of the extent of socialisation of sample respondents of working women is given in the following table.

TABLE – 4

Distribution of Respondents over the Extent of Knowledge of Names of Political Parties

N=60

Extent of Knowledge	*Number of Respondents*	*Per cent*
To a great extent	42	70
To some extent	12	20
To less extent	06	10
Not at all	00	00

Regarding the knowledge about the names of political parties, it is found that 70% of the sample working women have the political knowledge to a great extent. Hence, the political socialisation of the working women is nonetheless remarkable.

Working women are not interested even to be the members of voluntary organisations, which are non-political in nature and which are service-oriented. This is due to the fact that they find no time, as they have been overloaded by household chores and the burden of the work-place. Only 18 (30%) of the total sample respondents give positive answer to the question: "Are you a member of any voluntary organisation?" The socio-economic characteristics of these 18 respondents are given in the following table.

TABLE – 5

Socio-Economic Characteristics of the Sample Respondents Being the Member of Voluntary Organisations

N=60

Variables	*Components*	*Frequency*	*Percentage*
Age	21-30 years	00	00
	31-40 years	00	00
	41-50 years	04	22.22
	51 years and above	14	77.77
Occupation	Teacher	08	44.44
	Lecturer	08	44.44
	Doctor	02	11.11
	Executive	00	00
	Administrator	00	00
	Clerk	00	00
Income	Below Rs.1500/-	00	00
	1501-3500	04	22.22
	3501-5500	14	77.77
	5501 and above	00	00
Marital Status	Married	02	11.11
	Unmarried	16	88.88
	Divorcee	00	00

From the above table, it can be inferred that most of the sample respondents, who are members of the voluntary organisations, belong to the age group of 51 and above, they are either lecturers or teachers. They are unmarried and their monthly income is between Rs.3501 and Rs.5500/-. The working women of young age group, the executives, administrators and clerical women and the women of least and highest income-group do not become members of voluntary organisations. The married women are less interested to take part in voluntary organisations. This shows that political socialisation of elder working women belonging to educational services and of middle income group is greater than the other groups of working women.

The knowledge of one's own rights indicates the extent of one's socialisation. Therefore, a number of questions relating to the rights of women were asked to the sample respondents to know their extent of socialisation. The following table gives the picture of the extent of socialisation of the sample working women.

TABLE – 6

Distribution of Respondents (Education-wise) Saying "Yes" to the Following Questions

Question Items	*High School (09)*	*College (17)*	*University/ Tech. (34)*	*Total (60)*
Have you any idea about constitutional provisions for equality of men and women?	03 (33.33%)	11 (64.70%)	30 (88.23%)	44 (73.33)
Have you any idea about legal provisions for women?	00	07 (41.17%)	25 (73.52%)	32 (53.33%)
Do you know about maternity benefits for women?	02 (22.22%)	15 (88.23%)	32 (94.11%)	49 (81.66%)
Do you know about reservation of posts for women?	00	05 (29.41%)	32 (94.11%)	37 (61.66%)

The above table indicates that working women are very much aware of their own rights and privileges conferred by the Constitution and laws. &3.33% of the sample working women are aware of the constitutional equality of men and women and 81.66 per cent women know about the provisions of maternity benefits. But, regarding the laws for providing special facilities for women, only 53.33 per cent of women respondents have the knowledge. This shows that about the laws made from time to time relating to the special benefits to women, women respondents are less aware. Similarly, only 61.66 per cent of women even know about the legal provisions of reservation of posts for women in services. When the awareness is related to education, it is seen in the above table that as education level rises, awareness of the working women regarding the constitutional and legal provisions increases. There is a positive relationship between the education and awareness of working women.

Political values, orientations and attitudes are inculcated into the minds of individuals through a number of agencies, which are known as agents of socialisation. In the present study, one of the queries is to find out which of the agents socialise the sample respondents most. An attempt has been made to find out the relationship between the various agents of socialisation with age, education, income, occupation and marital status of the sample respondents. This has been given in the following table. The agents of socialisation are demarcated as family members, educational institutions, peer groups at work place, political institutions and mass media. In this context, the question asked was: "Will you please tell which of the following agencies have influenced you most, so far as your political information and ideas are concerned?"

TABLE – 7

Distribution of Respondents over the Question of Agents of Political Socialisation

Agents of Socialisation	*Frequency*	*Percentage*
Family Members	11	18.33
Educational Institutions	09	15.0
Peer Groups at Work-place	17	28.33
Political Institutions	02	3.33
Mass Media	21	35.0

The above table indicates that 35 per cent of women are being mostly socialised by mass media and the peer groups at work place are mostly socialising 28.33% of the sample women. The role of family members and educational institutions as socialising agents become lesser than the above two agents particularly, in the case of working women. The role of political institutions as socialising agents becomes very marginal in the case of working women. It is also found in preceding paragraphs that working women though, are quite aware of politics but they participate less in the decision-making body.

It is interesting to relate the socio-economic factors with the socialising agents.

TABLE – 8

Age-wise Distribution of respondents over the Question of Agents of Political Socialisation

Age / *Agent*	*21-30 (09)*	*31-40 (10)*	*41-50 (24)*	*51 and above (19)*
Family Members (11)	01 (14.28%)	04 (40.0%)	01 (4.16%)	05 (26.31%)
Educational Institutions (09)	02 (28.56%)	03 (30.0%)	01 (4.16%)	03 (15.78%)
Peer Groups at Work-place (17)	01 (14.28%)	02 (20.0%)	12 (50.0%)	02 (10.52%)
Political Institutions (02)	00	00	00	02 (10.52%)
Mass Media (21)	03 (42.85%)	01 (10.0)	10 (41.66%)	07 (36.84%)

When the relationship between age group and agents of political socialisation was studied in the present paper, it is found that larger number of sample women of age-group between 21-30 years (42.85%) and of the age group of 51 and above (36.84%) are being socialised by mass media. But, the peer groups at work place are socialising larger number of sample women of age group between 41-50 years (50%). It is interpreted that while middle-aged working women are in large number being socialised by peer groups, the women of younger and older age group are in large number being socialised by mass media.

TABLE – 9

Education-Wise Distribution of Respondents over the Question of Agents of Political Socialisation

Education / *Agents of Political Socialisation*	*High School (09)*	*College (17)*	*University (34)*
Family Members(11)	05 (55.55%)	03 (17.64%)	03 (8.82%)
Educational Institutions(09)	02 (22.22%)	03 (17.64%)	03 (11.76%)
Peer Groups at Work-Place(17)	00	04 (23.52%)	13 (38.23%)
Political Institutions(02)	00	01 (5.88%)	01 (2.94%)
Mass Media (21)	02 (22.22%)	06 (35.29%)	13(38.23%)

TABLE – 10

Occupation-Wise Distribution of Respondents over the Question of Agents of Political Socialisation

Occupation / *Agent of Political Socialisation*	*Lecturer/ Teacher*	*Doctor*	*Executive/ Administrator*	*Clerk*
Family Members (11)	07 (20.58%)	01 (9.09%)	01 (16.66%)	02 (22.22%)
Educational Institutions (09)	08 (23.52%)	01 (9.09%)	00	00
Peer Groups at Work-Place (17)	09 (26.47%)	08 (72.72%)	00	00
Political Institutions (02)	02 (5.88%)C0	00	00	00
Mass Media (21)	08 (23.52%)	01 (9.09%)	05 (83.33%)	07 (77.77%)

TABLE – 11

Marital Status-Wise Distribution of Respondents over the Question of Agents of Political Socialisation

Marital Status / *Agents of Political Socialisation*	*Married (35)*	*Unmarried (20)*	*Divorce (05)*
Family Members (11)	09 (25.71%)	02 (10.0%)	00
Educational Institutions (09)	03 (8.57%)	03 (15.0%)	03 (60.0%)
Peer Groups at Work-Place (17)	06 (17.14%)	10 (50.0%)	01 (20.0%)
Political Institutions (02)	00	02 (10.0%)	00
Mass Media (21)	17 (48.57%)	03 (15.0%)	01 (20.0%)

TABLE – 12

Income-Wise Distribution of Respondents over the Question of Agents of Political Socialisation

Income / *Agents of Political Socialisation*	*Below Rs. 1500/- (8)*	*1501-3500 (14)*	*3501-5500 (18)*	*5501 and above (20)*
Family Members (11)	05 (62.5%)	05 (21.42%)	05 (11.11%)	01 (5.0%)
Educational Institutions (09)	02 (25.0%)	04 (28.57%)	02 (11.11%)	01 (5.0%)
Peer Groups at Work-Place (17)	00	02 (14.28%)	06 (33.33%)	09 (45.0%)
Political Institutions (02)	00	02 (14.28%)	00	00
Mass Media (21)	01 (12.5%)	03 (21.42%)	08 (44.44%)	09 (45.0%)

When agents of socialisation were associated with the levels of education of sample respondents, it is found that large number of sample respondents having university education are being socialised by mass media (38.23%) and by peer groups (38.23%). Respondents having college education in good number are being socialised by mass media (35.29%), and respondents having high school education in large number (55.55%) are being influenced by family members. Hence, it is inferred that as education level increases, the impact of family as socialising agent at later years becomes decreased.

When income becomes associated with socialising agents, it is found that large number of women having income over Rs.5501/- are being socialised by mass media (45%) and by peer groups (45%). Working women having income between Rs.3501/- and Rs.5501/- in large number (44.44%) are being socialised by mass media. But, on the contrary, the low income group respondents in large number (62.5%) are being socialised by family members. Hence, as income increases, the impact of socialising agents like mass media and peer groups increases. Similarly, the working women respondents like executives/ administrators and doctors are being more socialised by mass media compared to the clerical category of respondents. So far as lecturer/teacher category respondents are concerned, family members, educational institutions, peer groups and mass media socialise them more or less equally. But to our surprise, the role of political institutions as socialising working women of any category is very marginal. Relationship between socialising agents and marital status of working women has been found out. While large number of married working women (48.57%) are being socialised by mass media, large number of unmarried working women (50%) are being socialised by peer groups and 60% of divorcee working women are being socialised by educational institutions.

When mass media are greatly socialising working women, it is interesting to know which type of mass media like newspaper, books and journals, radio and television are playing a major role for inculcating in the minds of women political values, attitudes and orientations. So, the questions were asked about the exposure of working women respondents to different categories of mass media. But the questions were asked only to those who are socialised by mass media. The response pattern is given in table no.13.

TABLE – 13

Distribution of Respondents over the Question of Exposure to Mass Media (Multiple Choice)

N=21

Types of Mass Media Media	*Regularly Frequency (%)*	*Sometimes Frequency (%)*	*Never (Frequency (%)*
Newspaper	11 (52.38)	08 (38.09)	02 (9.52)
Books and Journals	07 (33.33)	09 (42.85)	05 (23.80)
Radio	03 (14.28)	05 (23.8)	13 (61.9)
Television	18 (85.71)	02 (9.52)	01 (4.76)

The above table shows that 85.71% of women respondents who are exposed to mass media are watching television news and political discussions regularly and 52.38% of this category of respondents read newspaper regularly. Hence, newspaper and television are most popular mass-media to socialise working women. Books and journals are being used as mass media socialising agents only by the women hiving high level of education and working as executive/administrator and lecturer/teacher.

Political socialisation motivates one to take part in the political process known as political participation. Political participation provides legitimacy to the political authority and political system. The absence of it is known as political alienation, which is a negation to democracy. Therefore, the extent of political socialisation is determined by the attitude towards political participation of the individual. In order to know the extent of political participation of the working women, the following questions were asked to the sample respondents.

TABLE – 14

Distribution of Respondents on the Basis of Their Participation

N=60

Question on Political Participation	*No. of Respondents Saying "YES"*	*Per cent*
Do you belong to any political party?	13	21.66
Do you take part in campaigning during election?	15	25.0
Have you contested in any election?	00	00
Have you voted in any election?	53	88.33
Have you approached any political leader to convey your grievances?	17	28.33

The above table indicates that very less number of sample working women belong to political party (21.66%), take part in political campaigning (25%) or approach the political leader for any kind of help (28.33%). So far as these political activities are concerned, working women take minimal part and they are never interested to obtain political power. Perhaps, this is due to the fact that working women do not find time to participate in these political activities side by side with their jobs as well as household works. Or, it may be due to the fact that women have less role socialisation as participants in decision-making bodies. Nonetheless, a large number of sample working women respondents (88.33%) are conscious of their constitutional rights and duties to participate in the elections to exercise their franchise right. Thus, the socialisation of working women in the role of voter is to be noted.

To conclude, it may be pointed out that working women are having their first socialisation during the age of 18 to 22 years, the age of completion of college education. Therefore, in case of women, it is rather late socialisation. Moreover, it is found that, early socialisation of women respondents during their childhood depends upon the education of their parents and specifically, upon the education of mothers.

The extent of political socialisation of working women has studied by knowing their awareness about political personalities, political parties and the political process. Their knowledge about political personalities and political parties is quite high, but in the political process, their involvement is not so remarkable. They are conscious to a great extent of their rights and privileges and they exercise their voting right, but they take less part in decision-making bodies. When the question of agents of political socialisation comes to be analysed, it is found that mass media have greatest influence in socialising working women in general. Of the different types of mass media, television has got greatest socialising impact upon the working women.

REFERENCES

Aktar, S.S., D.M. Restorjee and F. Farroqui, 1969, Attitude Towards working Women , *Indian Journal of Social Work,* Vol.30 (1), pp.57-61.

Altekar, A.S., 1962, The Position of Women In Hindu Civilisation, Motilal Banarasi Dass, New Delhi.

Beauvoir, S.D., 1974, *The Second Sex,* (Translation), Penguin Books, London.

Beteille, Andre, 1975, The Position of Women in Indian Society, in Devki Jain (ed.) *Indian Women,* Ministry of Information and Broadcasting, New Delhi.

Desmukh, D., 1958, Women's Education , *Social Welfare,* Vol. 5, pp.6-10.

Devi, S., 1984, Development of Women's Education in Orissa , *Orissa Review,* Vol.XII (263), pp.49-59.

Feinstein, K.W. (ed.), 1979, *Working Women and Families,* Sage Publications, U.S.A.

Greenstein, F.R., 1972, Political Socialisation in *International Encyclopaedia of Social Sciences,* (ed.), by David L.Sily, Vol. 13, Macmillan Co. and The Free Press, New York.

Gupta, A., 1971, Problems of Working Women , *Yojana,* Vol. 15, pp.21-30.

Hyman, H.H., 1959, *Political Socialisation: A Study in Psychology of Political Behaviour,* The Free Press, London.

Ranston, S.A., (ed.), 1977, *Handbook of Political Socialisation: Theory and Research,* The Free Press, New York.

Siegel, R.S. (ed.), 1970, *Learning about Politics : A Reader in Political Socialisation*, Random House, New Delhi.

Singh, K.P., 1974, A Comparative Study of Attitudes of Working and Non-working Women Towards Women's Education and Employment , *Inter Discipline*, No.4, pp.3-9.

Srinivas, M.N., 1970, *The Changing Position of Indian Women*, Oxford University Press, Delhi

13

WOMEN IN INDIAN POLITICS

Ms. Jayashree Tripathy, O.F.S.

Political status of women can be defined as the degree of equality and freedom enjoyed by women in the shaping and sharing of power and in the value given by society to this role of women.

The Indian Constitution guarantees political equality through the institution of adult franchise and Art. 15, which prohibits discrimination inter alia on grounds of sex. It should be kept in mind that this recognition of political equality of women was a radical departure not only from the socio-cultural norms prevailing in traditional India, but also, from many of the advanced western countries.

The United States and the United Kingdom granted franchise to women only after World War I after decades of struggle by their women. Most other countries, eastern or western, conceded it only after World War II. Japan granted franchise to women in 1946; China in 1949. The exceptions were Thailand and Philippines, which granted a limited franchise, similar to the Indian case in 1932 and 1933 respectively. Amongst the West European countries, France granted franchise to women in 1945 and Switzerland in 1971.

In the case of India, the two major forces, which acted as catalysts in the achievement of political equality of women, were the National Movement and the leadership of Gandhiji.

who declared himself to be uncompromising in the matter of women's rights.[1] "Women must have votes and an equal legal status. But the problem does not end here. It only commences at the point where women begin to affect the political deliberations of the nation.", thus wrote Gandhiji in *Young India*.[2]

Any account of the Indian National Movement will be incomplete without assessing the role that women played for their self-emancipation by organising themselves into different associations at all levels for the fulfilment of their ideological or cherished goals and through their participation in the field of politics.

ORIGIN AND GROWTH OF WOMEN'S MOVEMENT IN INDIA

The participants in the women's movement in India hailed mostly from a small group of the urban educated families. They belonged to all major religious communities, but the upper caste Hindus outnumbered others. A vast majority of them joined the national stream and participated in the Swadeshi, Non-Cooperation, Civil Disobedience or Quit India Movement either being persuaded either by their husbands or family members. It is only very few of them, who joined politics on their own.[3] Our main perception here is that the women's movement developed because of male associational politics in the late 19th and early 20th century India.

The lead in launching women's associations to improve their status was given by men, who were active in Hindu reform associations – the Brahmo Samaj in the Bengal Presidency and Prarthana Samaj in the Bombay presidency. The spirit that lies behind the activities of the leaders of the associations was reformist and revivalist in nature. The male leaders of these organisations tried to infuse their female relatives with their favourite ideologies and exhibited their advanced outlook before the British officials.[4] These early organisations encountered a lot of social opposition and as a result, some association leaders took to the path of revivalism.

Raja Rammohun Roy had founded the Brahmo Samaj in 1882. Since then, the Brahmo Samaj, the Arya Samaj, the Ramkrishna Mission and the theosophical society did a lot for the women. The Arya Samaj called for a return to Vedic practices and promoted women's education on that basis. The Ramkrishna Mission and the Theosophical Society of India sponsored social service and educational institutions for women.

Attempts at mass mobilisation during the Swadeshi period paved the way for the participation of women in several ways[5], like distribution of pamphlets, boycott of foreign goods and formation of a number of women's organisations etc. As a result of the growing influence of the revivalist consciousness, several local organisations came into existence. Among them, we can mention the Hindu Ladies Social and Literary Club (1902) founded by Ramabai Ranade, the Gujrati Stri Mandal (1903), the Women Zoroastrian Association (1903), Seva Sadan and many others. The Muslims were however, slow to accept English education and their efforts in female education and associations did not begin until the 20th century. Still, local Muslim Women's Associations were founded in the early 20th century by upper class Muslim women in several cities.

The origin of the Indian Women's Movements in elite associational politics of the late 19th and early 20th centuries shaped the Indian women's movement in several important ways. Four characteristics reflecting the circumstances of origin can be identified: 1) male direction, 2) a concept of complimentary sex role, 3) absence of a radical onslaught on patriarchal base of Indian culture and 4) orientation towards elite representation and not mass mobilisation. The characteristics not only reduced opposition to the Indian women's movement, but also limited the improvement in the status of women that the Indian women's movement could achieve.[6]

Among women's organisations of national importance, the All India Women's Congress became a permanent organisation with local constituent conferences and annual sessions. By 1932, numerous sub-committees had been established within the educational and social sections: literacy, rural reconstruction, labour, indigenous industries, and text books. During the 1930s, the "Commission System" was utilised for several sessions. Under this system, delegates from each constituent organisation were divided into interest groups (commissions).

WOMEN IN THE GANDHIAN ERA

Gandhiji's entry into politics and his launching the Khalifat and Non-Cooperation Movement (1918-1922) encouraged the growth of women's movement. Responding to his call, women from different communities and from all walks of life came out to join the struggle as political campaigners. They also joined protest marches and demonstration, as constructive workers, participating in and often taking charge of the village reconstruction programmes, as workers in the cause of social and economic justice, working for the removal of untouchability and other forms of social oppression. The highly educated women mostly joined hands to spread literacy and develop self-reliance among the people. Women, who had spent their lives behind *Purdah* came out to fight orthodoxy, superstition and communal separatism.

Social legitimation for such activity was not forthcoming at first, but the women joined the men to fight in the movement. Events proved that without the co-operation of women, the freedom struggle would not have been so successful. Under Mahatma Gandhi's direction, the Civil Disobedience Movement and the Salt Satyagrah saw women in the forefront. There were women of the upper or middle class, leading shattered lives in their homes, peasant women, working class women, rich women, pouring out in their tens of thousands in defiance of government orders and police *lathis*. It was not only the display of courage, but what was even more surprising was the organisational power they showed.[7]

This kind of participation had a direct impact on the attitude of women. A meeting of representative women's organisations in 1930 drafted a memorandum demanding immediate acceptance of adult franchise without sex discrimination. It was turned down by the then British Government. But in 1931 Karachi Session of Indian National Congress took the historic decision, committing itself to political equality of women, regardless of their status and qualification.

The Government of India Act, 1935 increased the number of enfranchised Indians, made provision for the proportional suffrage rights of women and realised some of the previous qualifications. All women over 21 years of age could vote, provided they fulfilled the conditions of property and education.[8]

Independence brought the promise of actual liberation and equality. The Constitution pledged the nation to achieving a just society, based on the principles of equality and dignity of the individual, and proclaimed the right to political and legal equality as fundamental right of all Indians. The guarantee against discrimination in employment and office under the state opened the avenues to office of power and dignity.

WOMEN'S MOVEMENT AND THEIR CAMPAIGN FOR POLITICAL REPRESENTATION

Women's movement in India achieved success in the field of their political representation moreeasily as compared to their British and American counterparts. The Indian women's campaign had to pass through two phases. In the first phase extending from 1917 to 1928, the issues were female enfranchisement and eligibility for the legislature. In the second phase from 1928 to 1937, liberalisation of the terms of enfranchisement and increasing female representation in legislatures. The success of the women's movement depended on the extent to which coincidence between women's interests, the British government elite and the educated Indian elite in the Indian Legislative Council and nationalist associations was possible.

The initial reaction of both the British authorities and Indian elite to the women's suffrage demand was negative. The Indian elite very soon agreed to support the demand and within two years the British authorities acquiesced the idea of women's suffrage, if it were approved by the Indian provincial legislature. British officials at first discussed the idea of women's suffrage as unrealistic under Indian conditions. The demand was mentioned in the Montagu-Chelmsford Report. It was rejected by the South-based Franchise Committee and the Indian Provincial and Central Governments in 1918 and 1919.[9]

Sarojini Naidu planned to offer a resolution of women's suffrage at the Congress session in December 1917. Three provincial conferences, five provincial Congress Committees, the Indian Home Rule League, the Muslim League, and the Congress passed resolutions in support of women's suffrage during that year. An idea of the arguments made to the Indian political elite by the women leaders can be gained from their statements to the Joint Select Committee on the Government of India Bill in 1919. Annie Besant and Sarojini Naidu appeared before the Committee on the Government of India Bill in 1919.[10]

The association of the educated elite readily gave their support to the women's demand for suffrage. The reformers, revivalists and the Khalifat and Non-Cooperation Movements created an atmosphere favourable to women's uplift and public participation of women. While the women's movement was very successful in influencing the British and Indian political elite, it was very unsuccessful in mobilising women to vote.

The women in small number participated in the General Elections of 1923 and 1926. Kamla Devi Chattopadhyay, who contested 1926 Election as an independent candidate of WIA, lost to the Congress candidate. WIA organised deputation to government officials to ask that women be nominated to the Legislative Councils. These women were nominated Dr. Muthulakshmi Reddy in Madras, Mrs. Ahmed Shah in the United Provinces and Mrs. A.Kale in the Central Provinces.[11]

The second phase of the women's movement campaign began with the hearings of the Indian Statutory Commission (Simon Commission) in 1928. The women campaigned for an extension of women's franchise and increased representation of women in the legislatures. All important groups agreed with these demands and the issues of contention were on what terms should the extension be granted and on what terms should women be represented. The Congress and one faction of the women's movement (the equal rights faction) argued that political representation should be based on adult suffrage, and not on reserved seats. The other faction of the women's movement (the women's uplift faction) argued for special franchise qualifications and reservations of seats for women. The demands of the women's uplift faction fit into the strategy of representation being formulated by the British policy makers, and many of these demands were incorporated into the new constitution. The Nehru Report issued as a protest against the Simon Commission in August 1928 also contained several provisions that marked a change in nationalist strategy towards the political representation of women. There was a "Declaration of Fundamental Rights" which included a provision "men and woman shall have equal rights as citizens".[12]

When Gandhiji launched civil Disobedience Movement,

women participated on a much larger scale than they did in the non-cooperation movement. After Gandhi was arrested, Sarojini Naidu directed the Salt *Satygraha* until her own arrest. Picketing was declared unlawful by the government and much attention was focussed on the arrested and *lathi* charges on women satyagrahis. [13]

There were several elections held during the second phase of the Women's suffrage campaign. Although women's turnout increased over the period, the women's organisations themselves did not play an extensive role in electoral mobilisation, as they lacked the necessary organisational structure.

In the 1937 elections to Provincial Legislatures, both the male and female electorates were greatly expanded so that approximately 43 per cent of the adult males and 9 per cent of the adult females were enfranchised. As a result of 1937 elections, 56 women entered the legislatures; there were 41 seats reserved for women in the provincial legislative assemblies 10 women won unreserved seats and five were nominated to provincial legislative Councils. A majority of women who won were Congress candidates. None of the leaders of equal rights factions contested the election.

INDICATORS OF RESPONSE OF FORMAL POLITICAL INSTITUTIONS TO WOMEN'S EQUALITY

The Committee on the Status of women in India (CSWI) made an assessment of response by political parties and the electoral process to the principle of sex-equality. Starting from the Constituent Assembly leaders of all political parties accepted the principle of sex equality without any debate or objection.

Studies commissioned by the CSWI concluded that in reality no party had recognised women as a source of political support.[14] This view can be supported by an examination of women's participation in the electoral processes for which the parties are the main mobilising agents. An analysis of women's participation in the General Elections shows a steady rise in women's desire to exercise their franchise and a shrinkage of the difference between percentage turnout of male and female voters. The second significant feature is the marked variations in women's mobilisation as voters between a consistent record of high mobilisation (Kerala, Tamil Nadu) and some states being equally consistent in low mobilisation (Orissa, Madhya Pradesh). The variation indicates an inter-relationship between women's demographic and general status, their literacy, work participation etc. and their ability to participate in the electoral process.

An analysis of women's performance as candidates for elections however, shows a very low level of candidates with the exception of the general elections of 1980, and a virtually secular decline in the percentage of winners from over 50 per cent in 1962 to less than 20 per cent in 1980.[15] This data indicate a) persisting failure of all political parties to nominate women in substantial number, and b) a sharp increase in women's desire to play an active role in politics in recent years. Till the late seventies, however, no political party has made any serious efforts to understand this rising aspiration on the part of the women.

Marked change has been, however evident in the last decade. Women activists within some parties have forced greater attention to women's issues within their manifestoes and general activities, special appeals were being addressed to women during election campaigns and the leadership of most parties have been forced to take public position on women's issues as the protests from women's organisations have gained increasing public support. In terms of institutionalised efforts to censor obstacles to women's effective participation and in educating their members, cadres and general public on women's issues however, their response was varied.

As the legatee of the party which has steered the freedom struggle, the Congress has always stated its support for the principles of equality enshrined in the Constitution. Though the party particularly in recent years has developed a tradition of having a number of women holding party office and has been led by a woman for the last 17 years, women activists from outside the party complain, of lack of interest or support for women's issues from women within the Congress party. While individual party leaders have occasionally lent their support to women's demands, there is little evidence of any serious debate within the party of any activism on the part of women members. The Janata Party manifesto of 1977 contained the following paragraph:

> "Women constitute half of the population of our country. No progress is possible if their problems and interests do not receive due attention. The Janata party believes in the equality of all citizens. It will, therefore, ensure to women equal remuneration and equal opportunities in all walks of life".

A woman leader of the party who became increasingly interested in women's issues during the period when the party was in power admitted that there was no genuine "Political Will" in support of women within the leadership. It is upto us to generate the political will. We have to begin by making party women, women legislators, social workers and other educated women conscious of the real issues. Only when they start sharing power, will the party or the government develop the political will.

The Bharatiya Janata Party represents the conservative section in Indian politics and support for a culturally nationalist ideology. Its earlier manifestoes while promising increased property rights for women and members of their husband's family, emphasised that there should be "no fundamental change in the traditionally established principles of social organisations" and emphasised women's responsibilities to the family. While the women's front of the party organised demonstrations against crimes against women, it has persistently refused to co-operate with other .women's organisations in joining a common platform.

The CPI believes that only a socialist system can liberate women that women have a role to play in bringing about the social revolution and stands for equality in every sphere on national life through removal of legal disparities and disabilities in education and employment. There is however, no evidence of any institutionalised method of developing the party's understanding of women's issues.

The documents of the CPI(M) party and of its mass organisations however, reveal a greater awareness of women's problems as well as of the party's own failure to take up women's issues at all levels. Organisationally, the party had supported the formation a) of an all India Co-ordination Committee of working women with the Centre of Indian Trade Unions (CITU) following a National Convention and b) the All India Democratic Women's Association, a national body which brought State level organisations for the first time.

The 1982 Party Congress took note of the "spirit in the rise of women's consciousness and movement" and called upon the party to take initiative in promoting mass organisations of women and education of the entire party regarding its stance on the women's front.

MOBILISATION OF WOMEN BY THE POLITICAL PARTIES

The Parliamentary Parties started viewing women as a constituency in the eighties. This changing attitude of the parliamentary parties towards women is reflected in their election manifestoes, their attitude towards women candidates and their overall electoral strategies. In Andhra pradesh, at the time of the State Assembly election, the popular regional party of that time, Telugu Desam, promised land rights for women. Mrs Indira Gandhi made reference to "Stree Shakti" and Bharatiya Janata Party began advocating the revival of ancient Indian culture, eulogising mythological women characters. They also demanded a uniform Civil Code but from an anti-Mulsim angle rather than women's rights perspectives.

In the electoral process, we find two contradictory factors. On the one hand, we have few powerful articulate women leaders who are mainly elite and on the other hand we have large number of women who are mere rubber stamps. However, the elite women's political presence is derived from their relations with male politician husbands, brothers, fathers, father-in-laws. Between 1962 and 1996, the total number of women who contested the Lok Sabha (Lower House of Parliament) has increased from 68 to 491 and the number of women who were elected has increased from 35 to 44.

Increasing number of meetings, Shibirs, Welfare programmes, weekly meetings, national conventions are being organised by different political parties of their women cadres. Mahila Congress, BJP women's Front, Communist Party of India, Janata Dal and Shetkari Sangathana have all organised conventions to discuss women's problems. In terms of rhetoric on women, a lot is done as all of them are competing with each other to establish their credibility in the eyes of women. If the Congress Government brought out a half – baked National perspective Plan, the Janata regime camp of with women's Commission. In the process, Indian women have come on the political agenda of the country through various techniques like collective action and programmes of consciousness raising.

WOMEN IN THE POLITICAL PROCESS

The available data of women in political process show

that political participation has remained elusive for them. With the rising number of the electorate the percentage of women voters also went on rising constantly from 37.1% in 1952 to 60% in 1971 and since then there was a process of fall from 60% to 55.85% in 1977 and 51.22% in 1980. Many factors affect the voting pattern such as education, religion, caste, class, traditions, efforts of the political parties and political awareness.

An analysis of Table 1 presents a startling picture while the number of women contestants rose from 51 (2.72%) in 1952 to 86 (3.00%) in 1971, there was a sudden fall in 1977.

TABLE - 1

Women Legislators, Women Candidates Contested and Elected to the Lok Sabha from 1952-96.

Year	*No. of Women Candidate Contesting*	*No. of Women Elected*	*Total No. of Lok Sabha Seats*	*% of Total*
1952	51	23	499	4.70
1957	41	27	500	5.46
1962	65	34	503	6.88
1967	66	31	523	6.01
1971	86	21	521	4.05
1977	71	19	544	3.50
1980	142	28	544	5.16
1984	157	42	544	8.26
1989	189	28	525	5.30
1991	307	39	544	7.16
1996	491	36	543	6.61

Source: Encyclopaedia of Women in India, 1976 edited by Bik Vashishta, Delhi, 1976. *Rajya Sabha Who's who, Lok Sabha Who's who, Myron Weiner, India at the Polls,* Washington DC. American Enterprise Institute, 1978 and 68, Kum Kum Chanda, *"Women MPs Eve's Weekly,* March 10, 1979, PP. 20-21.

Only 71 (2.92%) contested. Bust just as graphs have been creeping up in other sectors in the eighties, in the Seventh Lok Sabha Election in 1980, the number rose to 142 (3.66%). In 1984 election, the number rose further to 157 (3.70%) in general. In 1996, 496 women candidates contested the election, the highest ever. The difference between male and female contestants has also shown a declining trend from 1977 to 1984 from 94.17% to 93.83% (in 19800 and to 90.23% in 1984, but the percentages are still abysmally low hardly 4 out of 100. Contesting elections is still a male preserve.

In the first four elections from 1952 to 1967, the percentage of women who contested and those who were elected was much higher than their male colleagues. From 1952 to 1967 the percentages for each corresponding election: 45.09, 65.85, 52.30 and 46.96. Those for the men during the same years were 25.56, 35.59, 23.95 and 21.25. But in 1971, there was a sharp fall to 24.41 from 46.96%, it rose slightly to 26.76% in 1977 but again fell to 19.71% in 80 to rise to 26.75% in 1984. The old political norms of the Gandhian era have been totally discarded in these decades of sharp competitive politics victory ensuring tremendous opportunities of money making by abuse of power. Women find themselves at a great disadvantage in this cut-throat political atmosphere. They do not find it easy to Marshall all the money needed to win and also adopt underhand means. Without strong support from a party, women hardly stand a chance of winning the election.

WOMEN IN DECISION MAKING POSITIONS

The number of total women Ministers has never risen above 8 in the Central Council of Ministers. During the period of the first Prime Minister, Pandit Nehru, an enlightened man, a champion of the cause of women, there were 7 women ministers in his Council of Ministers. From 1971 to 1977 it was just 4 each and in 1980 and 1984 it is 5 each. Except for 1977 when there were two women Ministers of Cabinet rank, there never has been more than one in this rank, and in 1977 and 1980 it meant the Prime Minister only. Most of the women ministers have been in the rank of State Ministers or Deputy Ministers. Except in 1962, the percentage of women Ministers has never gone beyond 10%. However, compared to women's percentage as contestants and elected members it seems to be on a slightly higher plane. State power being a male monopoly with just a few crumbs thrown to women as if they were poor relations is the reality, which emerges out of this analysis.

In the States too, it has not gone beyond 10% at any point of time there have not been more than 35 Ministers in all the States of India. There have been 7 State Chief Ministers till date whom one can count on fingers.[16]

Even in allocation of portfolios, women are allotted the Ministers of Social Welfare most of the time, only rarely a State Minister in Finance or a Cabinet Minister in the Ministry of Health. Most of these are Ministers whose allocations are the first to be axed in any crisis. Even when put into decision making positions, important portfolios are held back from them.

Ms. Saileja, the ex-Union Deputy Minister for Education, terms this under representation of women in Indian politics as "a Great Indian Irony", considering the fact that the country had one of the strongest Prime Minister, Mrs. Indira Gandhi.

This under-representation of women can be attributed to the great amount of conservation shown by all the political parties. First of all, women are not usually considered winning candidates. Secondly, the few that are ultimately selected are more often than not those who come from established political families or from the old ruling princely families. In fact, a majority of women who are actively engaged in politics have had either husbands or parents in politics.

There are notable exceptions like Margaret Alva, Miss Mamta Banerjee, and BJP's Uma Bharati. These politicians have joined politics out of choice and have risen up the ladder from the grassroots. And all of them have done well in their respective parties. Then there is a minuscule category of those, who, because of their background, films for instance – have been considered "winnable candidates" by their respective political parties and succeeded in getting elected to the national and state legislatures. "If the entry of women in politics is difficult, their acceptance in their parties, is more difficult" says Girija Vyas, ex-Minister of State from Janata Dal. She points obviously to the under-representation of women in the decision making structure of the parties and governments.

As far as the political parties are concerned, except the Congress, the Janata Party and BJP, no other national parties have any visible women wings. The conservative attitude of the parties is responsible factor for the virtual absence of women members in the supreme decision making apparatus of every Indian Party. Both the Communist Parties do not have any women in their Politburos. Women have been ignored in the seat distribution, as for example, in 1996 Lok Sabha elections; three per cent of party candidates were women.[17] What is worse is that unless the issues concern women, hardly any woman member has been entrusted by the party to introduce important bills on the floors of Parliament. A recent study shows that in between 1952 and 1989, whereas the male members of the Lok Sabha introduced as many as 328 bills, women members introduce only 26 bills. The corresponding figures in the Rajya Sabha during the same period was 191 and 13.[18]

RECENT TRENDS IN ELECTORAL PARTICIPATION OF WOMEN

Women's participation in election over the past four decades has confirmed the initial hopes placed by the Fathers of Indian Constitution. Certain aspects of this participation are as follows:

1. Ever since our First Election, the physical participation of women has been more than what is anticipated. It has been more than proportionate to their level of literacy and to their urban population figures.
2. The percentage of female participation has been more or less steadily increasing.
3. The gap in the turn out between men and women is getting more and more narrowed. According to all accounts, the women had turned out in great numbers and the probability is that the gap would have reduced further.
4. The percentage of female turn out has been the maximum, when the nation has been really boggled down by issues of corruption, one-party rule, future of parliamentary democracy, national unity and integrity. Issues, which have created anxiety in the nation as a whole and turned more men as well as women to express their verdict on the future course of events also, seem important. This shows women are getting more and more politicised.[19]

The politicisation is combined increasingly with a degree of political awareness, which is getting expressed not merely in terms of their mobilisation at the time of voting, but also in the way they cast their votes. It is now held by many psephologists that the women, no longer vote blindly, or like herds of sheep, as ordered by their men-folk. Many surveys of the recent elections showed that women had a mind of their own and exercised their votes independently.[20]

Equally important has been the delinking of illiteracy among women and their voting behaviour. Literacy among women has been the lowest, particularly in the rural sectors and among the lower castes and Harijans. This however, does not make them irrational, or indifferent to the political problems, on the other hand, most of the time, they have demonstrated that they are politically sensitive and well aware of the various issues confronting them.

It is unfortunate that the mobilisation of women by political parties and their leaders have been for opportunistic short term goals of winning the elections or other particularistic purposes, not for long term goals of social change for women. Further, they have treated the women for their quantitative votes, as supportive instruments for general purposes, rather than understanding and acknowledging their special interests and perspectives for an important quality of life for them.

There has been a steady increase in the number of women coming forward to contest the elections. However, the same can not be held of the number of women, who are getting elected. The trend has been irregular, significantly declining in the seventies.

One might mention here the findings of election watchers in the recent polls that more women were worried by issues of threat to national unity and integrity, communalism and personal laws, than to anxieties about price rise and democratic budget.[21] The spontaneous response of women housewives and educated middle class elite to rape and dowry murders and to teasing of girls is a positive proof that women's problems are evolving the active participation of women of all classes, castes and ages in the common fight against social evils.

Our review of the women's movement and its interaction with political process in India reveals the undercurrent of contradictions that characterise the understanding of women's role in the political process – both among the national leadership and the women's movement.

The women's movement began with the notion of women's rights to education, to property etc.. But, it also contained the germ of a desire on the part of women – to play some role in public life. This aspiration soon developed into the debate – social work, or women's needs vs. political action for the country's freedom. The debate often centred round the repercussions on result of interaction between the two.

The supportive role soon gave way to women's determination to play a full role, on terms of equality with men. Bowing to their determination, national leaders admitted them as full partners in the struggle and accepted complete equality in 1931. But the rationale behind this shift was never explicitly articulated or clarified with the result of continuing ambivalence with the women's movement and the leadership of the new nation.

The issue of women's political role in post-independence India has acquired three major dimensions.[22] The first, made possible by the constitutional guarantee of equality, is participation in the decision making institutions from the grass-roots to the national government. The second dimension is the operationalisation of women's rights, economic, social and political, to translate the constitutional promises into reality. After being dormant for over three decades, this aspect has resurfaced and is being pursued with some vigour by women's movement with varying degree of response from government, political parties, media and public. The legal framework provides a strong base in this case, making it rather difficult for any institution or political group to adopt or overtly negative stance to the demands of the women" movement. Besides, the growing mobilisation of women's organisation is increasing women's visibility as a potential force that may need to be tapped. The third dimension is the purpose of women's participation, the nature of the impact that may or wish to make on the political process and the manner in which they wish to achieve their aims.

There exists a close relationship between women's activities and the process of politicisation. Among the large number of women activists, two trends are clear. Women, who begin activism on women's right issues, begin to realise at some stage that they can not bring about needed changes without political action. The conversion of some of the professionally non-political groups bear testimony to this. On the other hand, women, who begin their activism under the general banner of political movement, begin to develop some consciousness regarding women's issues. This has been the case with quite a few of the younger activists. Both these trends confirm the fact, which is often overlooked in the development literature on women that the women's issue, if it is to be resolved by equality of rights and responsibilities, is basically a political one.

REFERENCES:

1. "It was the spirit of nationalism and the exigencies of the nationalist struggle that accounts for women's progress in South East Asia and there was a direct correlation between the two phenomena.", Urmilla Phadnis and Indira Malini (eds.), Status of Women in Selected Countries, (Unpublished volume prepared for the Committee on the Status of Women in India,1974), p.92.
2. Mahatma Gandhi, *Young India*, 17.10.1929.
3. Jana Matson Everett, *Women and Social Change in India*, Heritage, Delhi, pp.44-141.
4. Usha Chakraborty, *Condition for Bengali Women around the Second Half of the Nineteenth Century*, Calcutta, 1963, pp.98-106.
5. Sumit Sarkar, *The Swadeshi Movement in Bengal*, New Delhi, 1973, pp.115-116 and 271-288.
6. Jana Matson Everett, *op. cit.* pp. 65-68.
7. Jawaharlal Nehru, *The Discovery of India*, p.27.
8. This Act increased the number of women voters to more than 6 million from 315,000 under the Act of 1919, A.B. Keith, *A Constitutional History of India*, 1600-1935.
9. Quoted by Jana Matson Everett, *op.cit.* p.103.
10. Edwin S. Montague: *An Indian Diary*, ed. By Venetia Montague, London, W. Heinemann Ltd., 1930, pp.115-116. Beasant skilfully utilised Hindu revivalist ideas to agree women's franchise. She stated "Sex as a barrier only cause from the western systems" and claimed that, opponents of women's suffrage "object to the revival of old Hindu custom of recognising women's place in public life." The Tatas pointed to the

importance of women's uplift because of their role as mothers and educators of the next generation. In these presentations the women appealed to values that were held by the majority of the educated elite of the period.

11. Jana Matson Everett, *op.cit.*, pp. 111-112.
12. *The Nehru Report.*
13. Jana Matson Everett, *op.cit.*, pp.115-135.
14. *Report,* Committee on the Status of Women in India, "Towards Equality", 1975.
15. Vina Mazumdar (ed.), *Symbols of Power,* Allied Publishers, Bombay, 1979.
16. Prakash Nanda, "Hard Times for Women in Politics", *Times of India,* Dec. 3, 1994.
17. Devki Jain, "Women and Elections: Lost Opportunity", *Times of India,* May 2, 1996.
18. Prakash Nanda, *op. cit.*
19. Susheela Kaushik, "Political Participation of Women in India: Recent Trends", Paper presented in the Seminar held at CWDS, 1990
20. Chandra Bharill, "Political Participation and Indian Women", Paper presented in the Seminar held at CWDS, 1990.
21. Susheela Kaushik, "Political Participation of Women in India: Recent Trends", Paper presented in the Seminar held at CWDS, 1990
22. Vina Mazumdar, "Women's Participation in Political Life in India", Paper presented at the Seminar held at CWDS, Delhi, 1987.

14

WOMEN IN STATE LEGISLATURE: A CASE STUDY OF WOMEN IN ORISSA STATE LEGISLATIVE ASSEMBLY

Dr. Ramesh Chandra Mishra

Over the years since the U.N. Declaration of International Women's year in 1975, and its declaration in the same year of the decade for women, there has been a tremendous increase in national and international activities for advancement of the status of women. One of the most significant gains of the years following 1975 has been the generation of a world-wide ferment on the women's issues, representing "one of the most profound, quiet revolutions of our time".[1] And it has been rightly commented: "women's advancement has achieved a certain momentum.... It will also continue to exist as a force to be reckoned with...."[2] "There is discernible concern for making women participate in political, economic and administrative affairs".[3]

By now, as many as four world-conferences have been held on women: the first one was at Mexico in 1975; the second at Copenhagen in 1980; the third at Nairobi in 1985; and the fourth was held at Bejing in September 1995. But it has been found that nothing has changed significantly since the years before this spurt of activity commenced in the wake of the women's decade.[4] Of course, in some countries, equal opportunities movements have achieved formal political gains. Sweden was the first country to make in 1972 quota laws for political advancement of women. Argentina, Cuba and Venezuela have all established quota laws to ensure female representation. Costa Rica has promulgated a law for ensuring real equality for women. The world over, the participation of women in political decision-making is still, a symbolic one. From India to England, the percentage of women in the Parliament is seven to nine.

India's record on women in politics is never encouraging. The post-independence India created a new political order in which the constitutional infrastructure opened up equal political opportunities for all. But despite the constitutional promise of a political atmosphere free from discrimination of any kind, there exists a gender-discrimination, legally invisible though, in the realm of politics, largely because of the continuation of the in-built inhibitions of the Indian Patriarchal Society. Politics has traditionally been viewed as a male preserve.

The Committee on the Status of Women in India in its report (1975) recognised the problems of women in India and suggested some means for their advancement. The Indian Government in its *National Perspective Plan for Women* (1988) envisaged political and economic emancipation of women, and aimed at restoring to women their rightful place in society.

The Committee on the Status of Women in India had suggested reservations for women at the grassroots level of democracy and had urged political parties to field at least 15 per cent of women candidates for Indian Parliament and state Legislative Assemblies. The NPP (1988) in its original draft had proposed co-option of women into 30% of the seats in all representative bodies, from Panchayats to Parliament. But the NPP had to revise its original suggestion under pressure from women bodies and had to be satisfied with reservation of 30% of seats for women only in the Panchayat system. And in 1989 the 64th Constitution Amendment Bill sought

30% reservation for women in Panchayats. Karnataka and Andhra Pradesh introduced between 22 and 25 per cent reservation for women in Panchayats and Zilla-Parishads. The 73rd Constitution Amendment put more than 1,00,000 women in Panchayati Raj Institutions by incorporating the provision for 33% of seats reserved for women in the decision-making bodies at the local level.[5] And now in September 1996, the Indian government has introduced a Bill for reservation of 33% of seats for women in the legislatures. "In the 20 years since the Report (CSWI-1975) has been written parties have remained stubbornly unyielding on the question of fielding women candidates in the Lok Sabha and Assembly elections. Therefore, reservation has become an urgent imperative."[6]

Like elsewhere in the world, the change in the political status of women in India is largely cosmetic ".... Modern feminist movements have not been extensively instrumental in changing the overall perspective opening out unhindered opportunities"[7] Study reveals that through the ten Lok Sabhas the highest percentage of women representation have been 8.1% (8th Lok Sabha) and that to only 39 women in a House of 542. In case of Orissa's Legislative Assembly, the highest percentage of women representation have been 6.1% (10th and 11th Assemblies) and that to only 09 women in a House of 147. Male dominance in politics, thus, leads one to infer that there is a close relationship between sex and politics.[8]

There is a need of more in-depth studies bearing upon women's role in politics.[9] Improvement of the status of women is in large measure linked with their empowerment. Empowerment of women is meaningless without ensuring equal or adequate opportunities for women to take part in Legislative decision-making. Legislatures are the most enduring and widely applicable inventions of political man (K.C.Wheare). Legislatures in modern democratic political systems are still regarded as the most important formal centres of authority endowed with the privilege of "Authoritative allocation of values for society" (David Easton), or, as Lasswell says, of "deciding who gets what, when and how?".

Legislature remains the fulcrum of decision-making in all democracies. The importance of legislative studies, therefore, has increased in the recent decades; and studies made along newer methodological lines and have made innovative developments in research in Political Science. Legislative behaviour has become an important area of study, which has given rise much of the outstanding political behaviour research. The "Legislative Role" and the model methodology of legislative role-analysis, which emerged from the seminal work of Wahlke et. al[10] nearly made a breakthrough in the history of comparative legislative politics. Role-theory, as one seminal approach, studies legislature in its structural and functional perspective, and focuses on the individual legislator's behaviour in the Legislative system.

The present work is an abstract of the research study, made along the methodological lines of Wahlke et al., of the Role of women Legislators of Orissa based on the responses of women legislators of ten Orissa Legislative Assemblies. The justification of the decision in favour of a longitudinal study of ten Assemblies is the paucity of women in any one Assembly. The data and information used in the work are primarily from those collected through direct interviews, conversations discussions with related persons, and from other sources like the News Dailies, Orissa Legislative Assembly's who's who, O.L.A's. Research Wing files etc. This study mainly uses Nadel's[11] 'second method' of analysis of the respondents' own views on their roles.

Orissa came into being as a separate province on 1 April 1936. It became a federating state of the Indian Union with the coming into force of the Constitution of India in 1950. The Indian Constitution provides for parliamentary system of government at the Union and State levels. The history of the present Orissa Legislative Assembly is traceable as far back as to the year 1937 in which, as per the Government of India (Constitution of Orissa) order – 1936, the Legislative Assembly of the new born Orissa Province came into existence. The first pre-independence legislature of Orissa continued until 19 September 1945, and the second one, constituted on 18 April 1946, worked as the transitional-link Assembly until the first post-independence State Assembly was organised as per the provisions of the Constitution of India.

The first full-fledged Legislature of Orissa came into existence on 16 February 1952. Since then, Orissa has seen eleven Assemblies. Male-dominance has remained a constant feature of the composition of all Assemblies. There is a gross under-representation of women in it, as shown in the table below.

TABLE 1

Shows Women Representation in Orissa Assembly during 1952-95

Year	*Total House Strength*	*Women No.*	*% of Total Strength*	*Men No.*	*% to Total Strength*
1952	140	03	02.14	137	97.85
1957	140	05	03.57	135	96.42
1961	140	05	03.57	135	96.42
1967	140	05	03.57	135	96.42
1971	140	01	00.71	139	99.28
1974	147	04	02.71	143	97.27
1977	147	07	04.76	140	95.23
1980	147	05	03.40	142	96.59
1985	147	08	05.44	139	94.55
1990	147	09	06.12	138	93.88
1995	147	09	06.12	138	93.88
Total	1582	61	03.85	1521	96.15

Women representation as is clear from Table No. 1 in Orissa Legislature touched an all-time high, so far, in the Tenth and the Eleventh State Assemblies. It is slightly higher than 6% in 1990 and 1995 Assemblies, whereas it has been always marginal varying between a very low percentage of 0.71 in 1971 and a high percentage of 6% in the last two Assemblies. In terms of the legislative seats, of the total number of 1582 seats of the eleven state Assemblies, a meagre 61(3.8%) have gone to women. Legislative politics in Orissa is, thus, a men's game and the Legislature is a men's club.

SOCIO-ECONOMIC PROFILE OF THE WOMEN LEGISLATORS

Analysis of the socio-economic composition of political elite is believed to be essential to the understanding of their attitudes and policies.[12] As regards the age of the women legislators, study of nine Assemblies reveals that a majority (over 60%) of them belonged to the middle-age group.

Caste seems to be an important social attribute of the women members of Orissa Assembly. Study of the eleven Assemblies reveals that there is a clear high caste dominance in the women presence in Orissa Legislature. Women from either the S.T. or the S.C. communities remained under represented in the State Assembly. It was only in 1980 that women from S.T. community were elected to the State Legislature for the first time. So far, S.T. women have made their entry into Orissa Assembly thrice: in 1980, 1985 and 1995, while women from the S.C. community have been elected to the State Legislature only once in 1990. And one interesting finding is that there is a streak of royal blood in the women legislators of Orissa. Assembly-wise, women of royal blood are found present in all Assemblies, except in two, in 1971 and 1980. Furthermore, whereas it has not been possible for any caste group to completely monopolise the women group in the State Legislature, it was so in 1957 Assembly that all the women legislators were women of royal blood. Thus, a very important dimension of the caste composition of women legislative elite of Orissa is the preponderance of high-cast women.

As regards the parents and husbands of the women legislators, it is found that in the case of most of them one of the male members, either husband or father was active in politics. Husband in the case of many of them was a M.L.A or M.P. at different times. In some cases, father was a Freedom Fighter for the country. Most of the women legislators were from reasonably better educational backgrounds. And the father and / or husband of many of them belonged to high income-status. Thus, most Orissa women legislators belong to the top of the society's hierarchical structure.

MAKING OF THE POLITICAL WOMEN

Scholars[13] have stressed the need of linking the study of role-concepts of the legislators to their process of political socialisation chiefly because it gives the legislative actors to the political world. Political socialisation instills in the legislator the attitudes and pre-dispositions to politics which smoothens his induction into the political process. In the present work, the socialisation pattern of the Orissa women legislators is based on the findings from their own descriptions of when and how they acquired the lessons of political objects.

In a developing society like ours, the traditional social taboos, societal ideologies and myths associated with a patriarchal heritage prevent women from developing strong links with the wider network of social contacts. Women's environment tends to act as a barrier to political stimuli, so restricting the likelihood that they will participate in politics.[14] It is also a fact of general experience that "women in many societies are prone to be adversely affected by dominant societal ideologies and predilections and, consequently become captive of self-alienation simply because, first, they are socialised to acceptance of a culture of domination by the male, and the compliance thereof becomes a matter of behavioural and attitudinal given; second, women themselves become the prime movers of oppression against women, and male domination is thus further compounded."[15]

Study of the respondents' views reveals that a majority (55%) of them developed the itch for politics between their childhood and adolescent years. And though no comparative analysis could be made because of inequality in the proportion of caste-groups in our sample population, it would not be out of place to say that in more high caste women, the urge for politics sprouted in the early years of their lives.

Political behaviour is not congenital or instinctive. It is mostly learned. Political socialisation, like all learning, is imbibed from interaction between the learners and certain elements of his human environment called socialising agents or sources. In the case of a majority (54.5%) of the respondents, family was the socialising agent, whereas a good proportion (23%) were found socialised through their participation in India's Freedom Struggle. A minority (14%) reported that the state leaders influenced them, whereas a small minority (only 9%) revealed that they had personal inclination to politics. Hence, in classifying all the respondents into two broad types, as Cunningham[16] has done, it is seen that while most of the women legislators belonged to the kind of persons "who allowed themselves to be persuaded", a small minority (9%) of them were women "who (had) the itch of politics in their blood". Again, all of those who had the 'itch of politics' in their blood belonged to the high-caste.

On further analysis, it is found that those who developed interest in politics earlier had their chief source of interest in political participation, whereas, those, whose interest in politics was a result of persuasion by others had late development of concern for politics. Women from socially high parental families developed urge for politics earlier than others. Most of the women who had politically active fathers were socialised within the family circle, and those who self-started in politics were from high-income status families. For most of those who were late in development of political awareness, contribution of their husbands towards making them sensitive to politics was perceptible.

THE POLITICAL ASCENT : RECRUITMENT

The pattern of legislative recruitment provides a salient area of research in the analysis of the role-behaviour of legislators in so far as the mode of their entry into the legislative arena is believed to be impinging their role-concepts. As recruitment is characterised by sequence of events spread over the entire process of selection of those who exercise the ultimate power at the highest decision-taking level, a close look at the patterns of recruitment is relevant to understanding the nature of politics in which political mobility takes place.

In almost all democracies, it is the tide of opinion, which really carries some 'from among those who are politically active' to the Legislature through an elaborate process of election, though the whole phenomena amidst which political parties largely govern this work. In developing systems like India, recruitment, no doubt, has been reconciled to some traditional principles like the Indian provision of reservation of legislative seats for Scheduled Castes and Tribes.

Political antecedents often help in the final stage of legislative recruitment. Recruitment is believed to be preceded by some pre-legislative experience. Therefore, study of the responses of the legislators reveals that a majority (77%) of them had some kind of experience in public life before their entry into the Legislature. There does not emerge any single kind of experience as distinctly favourable to upward political mobility. But, pre-legislative incumbency in elective public offices does not see to be the pre-condition for elevation to legislature in most cases.

"The world of politics is very largely the world of political parties" (Conningham). The process of recruitment may vary from one political system to another according to whether there is single party non-competitive system or multi-party system, but political parties remain central to recruitment in almost all systems. In India, both at the national and the regional levels, the multi-party system operates in an environment of democratic competition.

The National and the regional parties in Orissa occupy a central position in the whole process of candidate recruitment, which precedes the final recruitment through. Study of the role of the political parties as agents of candidate-recruitment in the last ten elections to the State Legislative Assembly, it is clear that party has the most important role in political recruitment of women. In seven out of the ten elections (1957 to 1995), party-supported candidates far outnumbered the self-starters i.e. the Independents. It was only in 1977 and 1980 elections that the self-starters were more than the party-sponsored candidates. Furthermore, on reflection it is found that of the respondents who were interviewed, 95.45% were party-sponsored candidates. Hence, a party is the only important agent of recruitment of women into state Legislature. Parties have been playing the role of the actual 'gate-keepers' in the political rise of women in Orissa.

Again, women in Orissa also do not enjoy any specific support base, It is the parties which help them in obtaining electoral success. Study of the last ten Assembly elections reveals that it is the party sponsored women, who win the election. There are of course, two exceptions: in 1977 elections there was one independent woman candidate who was successful; and in 1985 there was another who was elected to the Assembly.

As regards caste-based support, high-caste women do

not rely on caste support whereas the S.T. and S.C. women find it convenient to make full use of caste-support in elections. Caste-constituency provisions have turned caste into a significant support base in elections.

One very interesting aspect of Orissa Elections is that the women from former princely families enjoy an added advantage compared to other high-caste women candidates. Though many of the women of royal blood belong to families, which in the past did not favour democratisation of Orissa polity, they took all the advantages of democracy and turned the traditional allegiance of a sizeable proportion of the electorate to the royal families into electoral support.

In most cases of the women in Orissa politics, their acceptability to the political parties was much less a problem in view of the popular support and political influence their husbands and / or fathers commanded in the electoral areas. Political parties also picked up women from politically influential families in which, at least, a male member held at sometime elective office in State or Union legislature or took part in India's freedom struggle. Parties intended to politically encash the image, which these families had built over the years of their political toil. Thus, behind the formal leadership of the political parties in the recruitment of women was the reality of the latter's family connections which not only helped them in being chosen as party candidates in elections but also provided the political climates favourable to gaining entry into state Legislature.

OPPORTUNITY STRUCTURE

Since opportunities, as circumstances and occasions are lined with the recruitment process, study of the former is necessary. The notion of opportunity structure[17] basically implies the picture of imminence of political vacancies in a relatively institutionalised infrastructure of roles and positions.

Though the ascent of an individual in the political hierarchy may be facilitated to some extent by his advantageous location in the socio-economic set-up, it is by no means solely dependent on those socio-economic variables, but on the other hand, also much depends on how one uses the opportune situation for his upward mobility. There is no certainty as to the kind of situations one would encounter, but there is, apparently, an uniformity in the behaviour of the aspirants in their attempt to turn such situations into boosters to their struggle for office. "In political activity, then, men sail a boundless and bottomless sea; there is neither harbour for shelter nor floor for anchorage, neither starting place nor appointed destination. The enterprise is to keep afloat on an even keel; the sea is both friend and enemy; and the seamanship consists in using the resources of a traditional manner of behaviour in order to make a friend of every inimical occasion."[18]

Thus, what distinguishes the politically active ones or the political eligibles[19] from common citizenry is the adroitness with which the former utilises the political opportunities as and when they surface, whether, as Marvick[20] observes, in the form of 'discrete' opportunities springing up as products of chance or in the form of 'sequence' of opportunities, which the political environment creates.

Independence in India brought in its wake a vast number of public offices as a result of democratisation and decentralisation of power, and, at the same time, abolished the traditional social status structure. This contributed to a rush for political offices in India.[21] Analysis of the responses of the women legislators shows that little more than 68% of them entered the legislative arena by using opportunities created by their family members. And most of them availed of 'discrete' kind of opportunities which chance or accident offered to them.

The opportunity structure studied together with the important role of political parties in recruitment of women in Orissa reveals yet another interesting dimension of political ascent of women in Orissa. In some cases, especially in 1985, 1990 and also in 1995 elections, the recruitment pattern seems to be a sort of hereditary succession of women to the political throne of their husbands. Political parties seemed to have been reconciled, to a great extent, to the principles of dynastic politics or to what is called, the "feudal conditions of democracy".[22] ".... A woman is automatically chosen to contest an election only when she is seen as a symbolic continuation of her husband."[23] In India, in Orissa too, a good proportion of women in politics (e.g. 5 in 1985, 5 in 1990 and 2 in 1995) can be called "Suttee Careerists"[24] who "carry on a public life in place of a dead or otherwise absent husband or father".

ROLE OF THE WOMEN LEGISLATORS

Study of the self-perceptions of the legislators about their roles in the legislative structure assumes importance in legislative research in view of the limitations[25] of the study of their overt performances to know their actual legislative roles. It is argued that there can be no real assessment of the legislator's role orientations from their overt actions as observable performances are always limited to a particular stage in the legislative process and confined to a particular location in the large size of the legislative bodies. Overt performances may be misleading, as legislative politics is secretive in character.[26]

Since a legislative role is taken in an interaction situation, legislators develop roles primarily as in relation to fellow legislators, as in reference to the core-functions of the legislative system, and as in response to the legislator's various clienteles like the electoral constituents, the party, the pressure groups, etc.

Study of the respondent's own perceptions of their roles in the variety of sectors of the legislature leads to significant findings about the legislator's role-orientations in reference to purposive, representational, and real activities. It also reveals the mind of the legislator about her relation with the represented members and with the women.

LEGISLATIVE PROCESS AND THE PURPOSIVE ROLE

Purposive roles refer to the roles taken by legislators in the central area of legislative activity, which reflect the purpose of their legislative participation. The legislator's self-perceptions of the type of behaviour, which he or she would demonstrate in articulating the interests and in shaping the public policies reveal their orientations to the central area of legislative activity – the core roles sector.

TABLE - 2

Distribution of Respondents over the question of perception of their purposive Roles.

Role Orientations	*Total No.*	*%*	*High Caste N=16*		*S.T. N=6*	
			Number	*%*	*Number*	*%*
Tribute	16	72.72	10	62.50	06	100.00
Ritualist	01	04.54	01	05.25	00	—
Inventor	02	09.09	02	12.50	00	—
Broker	03	13.63	03	18.75	00	—
	22	99.98	16	100.00	06	100.00

It is noticeable from the above table that Tribune role receives the largest number of mentions among the respondents. It shows that most women legislators are interested in articulating and defending the popular demands (Tribune–orientation). Nearly 73% of the respondents indicated Tribune - role – orientation, which means they think themselves as guardians and defenders of people's interests. Only a small minority (one) laid more emphasis on the rituals of the legislative process (Ritualist) rather than on legislative goals. Legislators who believe in formulating public welfare policies (Inventors) constitute a mere 9%. And Brokers, who try to integrate or harmonise the divergent demands made upon the legislature, constitute 13.63%. Significantly, there are no Ritualists, no Inventors, and no Brokers among the S.T. women of the State Assembly.

Thus, in the legislature's central area of activity, the Orissa women members believe protecting and promoting popular interests as to be the ultimate aim of their legislative functions.

REPRESENTATIONAL ROLE

Finer[27] has linked representation to responsibility and to the popular will to 'make and unmake governments'. Wahlke et. al. interpret the role of the representative as in terms of the link between the representative's style and focus of decision-making, and the expectations of the represented. Though, the 'represented' recognise the legislative decisions as legitimate and authoritative because of the socially and legally approved manner of election, considering the functional consequences of representation, it is argued that popular acceptance of the legislative decisions is more due to the reason that the ways in which these decisions are taken are in accord with the expectations and demands of the represented.

Much of Wahlke et al.'s theoretical interpretation is based on Burke's[28] theory of representation, which believes that the legislator is a free agent who concentrates on the interest of the whole nation. The idea of free-agency is related to the style of representation, whereas the idea of a single 'whole' national interest refers to the focus of representation.

Table 3 shows the result of a probe into the minds of the respondents regarding their representational style role-perceptions. The responses analysed in the manner, as shown in the table below, indicates that a clear majority (64%) of them exhibited "Delegate" orientations, which means that the respondents perceive themselves as being guided by the mandate of the represented. Slightly over a quarter of them viewed themselves as "Trustees", who set as free agents, whereas, a little less than a tenth of them projected "politics" orientations, which means a compromise between the Delegate and the Trustee orientations.

TABLE - 3

Showing Distribution of Respondents over the Question of Perception of their Representational Style Roles.

N – 22

Represent-ational Style	*Total* No.	%	*High Caste* No.	%	*S.T.* No.	%
Trustee	06	27.27	06	37.5	000	—
Delegate	14	63.63	08	50.00	06	100.00
Politico	02	09.09	02	12.50	00	—
	22	99.99	16	100.0	06	100.00

It becomes clear that most women legislators in Orissa set in tune with the demands and instructions of the people. And, whereas a half of the high caste women feel themselves as following the mandate of the people, all the S.T. women do so. But at least half of the high caste women in the legislature perceive themselves as free agents following their own of those who believed themselves as free agents, also, perceived themselves as 'mentors' of the people.

Further analysis of the responses to find out interpenetrational relations between the legislators' Representational style and Purposive role orientations, it is exhibits that 86% of the Delegates and 67% of the Trustees are Tribunes in their Purposive. Orientations, all Politicos are Brokers.

Thus, what is common to both, those who viewed themselves as carrying out the instructions of the people and those who projected themselves as free-agents, is the defence of the people's interests.

AREA OF ATTENTION: THE AREAL ROLE

The Areal Role refers to the focal aspect of the Representational role which corresponds to the legislator's own definition of the constituents he represents. Generally, legislators view representation of the interests of some geographical area as a vital part of their legislative functions.

TABLE - 4

Showing Distribution of the Respondents over the question of perception of their Representational Areal Roles

N = 22

Represent-ational Focus	*Total*		*High Caste(N=16)*		*S.T. (N=6)*	
	No.	*%*	*No.*	*%*	*No.*	*%*
Electoral Constituency	15	68.18	11	68.75	04	66.66
State	05	22.72	05	31.25	00	—
Both	02	09.09	00	—	-02	33.33
·	22	99.99	16	100.00	06	999.99

It is evident from the above table that quite more than two-thirds of the women legislators are constituency-oriented. This suggests that for most of the women legislators, constituency interest is the focus of their legislative actions. Whereas, there is a good proportion (31%) of high caste women who are oriented to the general interests of the State, there are no such women among the S.T. legislators. The only two women who try to bring a balance between the State and the Constituency interests in the legislature belong to the S.T. Community.

On analysis, a trend seems to emerge from linking the

Representational style and Areal role orientations. Clearly an overwhelming majority of Delegates tend to be constituency-oriented and an exact two-thirds of Trustees are found to be State-oriented.

OMBUDSMANIC ROLE

A chief consequence of the process of modernisation of the legislatures and of the interaction of the legislature with its environment is the legislator's increasing non-legislative engagements like constituency works.[29] The legislator's constituency role stems not only from his being both an outsider and an insider, but also from the people's expectations and demand that the representative be available to the constituents in personal and collective matters. Almond and Verba (The Civic Culture, 1963) have seen that in U.S. and in U.K. Constituents turn more often to the legislators in case they are aggrieved or in difficulty. Barker and Rush (1970) observed this trend to be "... an important part of modern British political culture". In the modern context of expanding government services and activities, individuals are likely to be more affected and it is observed[30] that ".... The more they are affected by government the more they seem to turn to their elected representatives as a source of help in dealing with the government". In the Indian context, scholars find out almost the same thing. Bailey[31] observes: "He (the M.L.A.) is, therefore, to direct benefits in the direction of his constituents, to help individuals to get what they want out of administration and to give them a hand when they get into trouble with officials". And basing on the Swedish idea of the complaint-handling nature of the constituency works of the legislator, such a role has been typified as the ombudsmanic role. Mohapatra[32] has identified such a role of Orissa Legislators.

The analysis of the perceptions of the respondents establishes that an amazingly high (86.36%) proportion of Orissa women legislators believe themselves as performing some sort of Ombudsmanic role. It is found that the legislators encounter demands both of purely personal and collective nature from their constituents. And mostly, they sort them out through three ways: contacting the concerned authorities; raising the matter in the legislature; and mobilising public opinion in favour of the issues.

WOMEN INTERESTS AND WOMEN LEGISLATORS

The Committee on Status of Women in India in its Report (1975) mentioned that women Legislators did not perceive themselves as leaders addressing exclusively to women issues. Jahan[33] observes that women legislators do not identify themselves with problems that affect women specifically.

In our enquiry to know as to in what measure do women leaders hold women issues as important to them, it is found that though, nearly 80% of the respondents admitted that they receive requests for help in special women issues, their efforts to handle them are primarily limited to words or, speeches either inside or outside the legislature. Nearly 41% of the respondents did not know what to say in answer to our question about their endeavours to advancement of the women's cause.

Most of the women legislators perceived the interests of the constituents to be inclusive of the women interests. Thus, though women legislators of Orissa feel that they have some women-interest role to play, they have not been able to identify themselves with problems that affect women specifically.

REFERENCES

1. Neerja Choudhury, "The Women's Decade-I" in *The Statesman*, Calcutta, 18, September, 1985.
2. *Forward Looking Strategies for Advancement of Women to the year 2000 A.D.*, Report of the Nairobi World Conference, July 1985.
3. Sushila Patri, *Women Political Elites: Search for Identity* (Jaipur: Printwell, 1994), p.1.

4. *Forward Looking Strategies*......July 1985.
5. Ruchira Gupta, "The Rocky Road to Gender Equality", *The Times of India*, New Delhi, 24 September 1996.
6. *Ibid.*
7. Sushila Patri, *op. cit.*
8. Lionel Tiger, *Men in Groups* (Landon, Nelson, 1969), pp. 12-13.
9. Jane S. Jaquette, *Women in Politics* (N.Y.: John Wiley and Sons, 1979)
10. John, C. Wahike, heinz Eulau, William Buchanan, and Le Roy C. Ferguson, *The Legislative System* (N.Y.: John Wiley & Sons, 1962)
11. S. F. Nadel, S. F. Nadel, *The Theory of Social Structure* (Glencoe, Illinois: The Free Press, 1957), p.25.
12. Harold D. Lasswell, Daniel Lerner and E. Rothwel, *Comparative Study of Political Elites* (Stanford: Stanford University Press, 1952); D.R.Mathews, *The Social Background of Political Decision-Makers* (Garden City, N.Y.Double Day, 1954). Rounaq Jahan, "Member of Parliament in Bangladesh", *Legislative Studies Quarterly*, 1,3 (August 1976).
13. Herbert Hyman, *Political Socialisation* (Glencoe, illinois, 1959); Lesswell, *op. cit.*, Michael Rush and Phillip Althoff, *An Introduction to Political Sociology* (N.Y.: Indianapolis: The Bobbs – Merrill Co., 1972), p.17.
14. L.W.Milbrath, *Political Participation* (Chicago : Rand Mc Nally, 1965) . p.39.
15. Maurice Duverger, *The Political Role of Women* (Paris: UNESCO, 1955), p.25-26 : An Except from Sushila Patri, p.4.
16. George Cunningham, *Career in Politics* (London: Kogan Page, 1984), p.12.
17. Joseph A. Schlesinger, *Ambition and Politics* (Chicago: Rand Mc Nally, 1966).
18. Michael Oakeshott, *Political Education* (Cambridge : Bowes and Bowes, 1951), p.22.
19. L.G. Seligman, *Recruiting Political Elites* (N.Y.: General Learning Press), 1971.
20. Dwaine Marvick, "Continuities in Recuritment Theory and Rearch" in Heinz Eulau and M. Czudnowski(eds.) *Elite Recruitment in Democratic Politics* (N.Y.: Halsted Press, 1976).
21. Myron Weiner, "India : Two Political Cultures" in Pye and Verba (eds.) *Political Culture and Political Develcpment* (New Jersey, Princeton : Princeton University Press, 1972).
22. Tavleen Singh in *The Sunday Times*, London, 24 January 1988.

23. Rashmee Z Ahamed, "Suttee Careerist" and Good Housewives" in *The Times of India*, New Delhi (National Edition), 4 October 1996.
24. *Ibid.*
25. Wahlke et. al., *The Legislative System*, op.oit.,pp.238-240.
26. *Ibid.*
27. Herman Finer, *The Theory and Practice of Modern Government* (N.Y. : Holt, Rinehart and Winston, 1959) p.219.
28. Edmund Burke, "Speech to the Electors of Bristol" (1974), *Works – II* , p.12.
29. Anthony Barker and Michael Rush, *The Member of Parliament and His Information* (London : Allen & Unwin Ltd., 1970); Raymond F. Hopkins, *Political Roles in a New State* (New Haven: Yale University Press, 1971).
30. David M. Olson, *The Legislative Process* (New York : Harper and Row, 1980), p.135.
31. F.G. Bailey, *Political and Social Change : Orissa in 1959* (Berkeley: University of California Press, 1963).
32. N. K. Mohapatra, "Ombudsmanic Role of the Legislators in an Indian State", *Legislative Studies* Quarterly, August, 1976.
33. Rounaq Jahan, "Women in South Asian Politics", *Third World Quarterly*, July 1987.

15

AETIOLOGY OF GENDER GAP IN POLITICAL REPRESENTATION OF ORISSA

Dr. Urmimala Das

Political institutions are one of the most masculines of all institutions into which women may not easily integrate. Gender based subordination is deeply ingrained in the consciousness of both men and women and is usually viewed as a natural corollary of the biological differences between them. It is reinforced through religious beliefs, cultural practices and educational systems and political processes that assign to women lesser status and power. Equality in political participation and decision making is one of the major priorities for women liberation. Without success in this area, other areas of development of women will be but at risk.

Political culture of women in Orissa has its roots in its state formation process where women play very little role, close to invisibility. Again when women constitute 49% of state's total population, they are scarcely represented in its political leadership. As citizens, they have the civil and political right and responsibility to participate fully in their state and national politics, but they do not. Some aspects of this situation are outlined below.

This paper focuses on the active and organised participation in politics of women collectively and includes such matters as participation of women of Orissa in elections as candidates to various legislative bodies.

TABLE – 1

Women MLAs' in Orissa (1937-90)

Sl. No.	*Year of Assembly Elections*	*Total Strength of the Assembly*	*No. of Women Elected*	*Elected Women Legislators in Percentage*
1.	1937	60	2	3.3
2.	1946	91	3	3.3
3.	1951-52	140	3	2.1
4.	1957	140	5	3.8
5.	1961	140	5	3.8
6.	1967	140	5	3.8
7.	1971	140	1	0.7
8.	1974	140	4	2.9
9.	1977	147	7	4.8
10.	1980	147	5	3.4
11.	1985	147	8	5.4
12.	1990	147	9	6.1
13.	1995	147	9	6.1
	Average			3.4

Source: Women Legislators in Orissan Legislative Assembly, 1937 – 90.

Table 1 unravels the women's representation in State Assembly. In Orissa, though women constitute half of the total population but they have not been able to get adequate representation in state legislature. 5.4% is the highest percentage. This is not a peculiar trend for Orissa only because it is also the case of India as a whole.

Of the 10 Elections held in post-independence Orissa, only twice the State Government was headed by a woman, Mrs. Nandini Satpathy. Except this in no other election, a women has held a ministerial-level decision making position. Mrs. Basanta Manjari Devi held the Ministry of Health in 1957. These two cases are exceptional. Though they have been able to breakdown some amount of the barriers and reduce overt male opposition; still many obstacles remain to be overcome before becoming an equal and visible party to decision making process. Moreover these two lady ministers had culturally the same background, access to formal education at an appropriate level, exposure to public speaking and to political issues. To start at the grass-root level Mrs. Nandini Satpathy's (Chief Minister) confidence to be a political leader was much a contribution of her political parenting and affluent background which assured her the contacts that had continued in later part as an invaluable net-working system. These exceptional cases can give no basis for generalisation. Above all they were integrated into existing male system and exclusively were not fighting for women's cause.

Table – 2

Percentage of Women Legislators in Lok Sabha.

Year of Election	*Percentage of Women Legislators*	
1952	4.4	
1957	5.4	
1962-67	6.7	From 1980 the gap has increased
1967	5.9	but not more than 10%.
1971	4.2	
1977	2.3	

Source: Women and Development CWDS, New Delhi, p.14

Table 3 confirms the above proposition for most of the women M.LAs of Orissa. 29 out of 56 M.LAs are from royal families and royal castes; were 18 come directly from royal culture. They have inherited the political culture of the family. 9 women are from Schedule Tribes group mostly representing from their reserved seats.

TABLE – 3

Caste Structure of Women MLA's of Orissa

No. of Assembly	*Roya Caste/ Family*	*Brah-min*	*Karanas*	*Khan-dayats*	*ST*	*SC*	*Telugu*	*Christian*
1937 (1st)	1	—	—	—	—	—	1	—
1946 (2nd)	1	—	—	—	—	—	1	1
1952 (1st)	2	1	—	—	—	—	—	—
1957 (2nd)	2	3	—	—	1	—	—	—
1961 (3rd)	1	3	—	—	1	—	—	—
1967 (4th)	—	4	—	—	1	—	—	—
1971 (5th)	—	—	1	—	—	—	—	—
1974 (6th)	—	1	1	1	1	—	—	—
1977 (7th)	1	3	1	1	1	—	—	—
1980 (8th)	—	—	1	—	—	4	—	—
1985 (9th)	—	1	1	—	—	5	1	—
1990 (10th)	3	2	1	1	—	1	1	—
Total	11	18	6	3	4	10	4	1

Table 4 indicates the district-wise distribution of women MLAs. Developed districts like Cuttack and Ganjam have been represented by 19 and 12 candidates respectively leaving aside the question of reserved seats.

TABLE – 4

District-wise Distribution of Women M.L.As 1937-90

Districts	*Pre-Independence*		*Post Independence*										*Total*
	1	2	1	2	3	4	5	6	7	8	9	10	
Balasore	—	—	—	—	—	1	—	—	—	—	1	1	3
Bolangir	—	—	—	—	—	—	—	—	—	—	—	—	—
Phulbani	—	—	—	—	—	—	—	—	—	—	—	—	—
Cuttack	1	1	3	2	1	1	1	2	3	1	1	2	19
Dhenkanal	—	—	—	1	1	1	—	—	—	—	—	2	5
Ganjam	1	2	—	1	1	—	—	1	2	—	1	3	12
Koraput	—	—	—	—	—	—	—	—	—	3	3	—	6
Mayurbhanj	—	—	—	—	—	—	—	—	—	1	1	—	2
Sambalpur	—	—	—	1	1	1	—	1	1	—	—	1	6
Sundergarh	—	—	—	—	—	—	—	—	—	—	1	—	1
Puri	—	—	—	—	1	—	—	—	1	—	—	—	2
Kalahandi	—	—	—	—	1	—	—	—	—	—	—	—	1
Total	2	3	3	5			1	4	7	5	8	9	57

The average participation of women in State Assembly was 3.4% during last 12 elections of Orissa (see Table – 1). This is the case perhaps because, to many women, politics is a vague expression of the meaning of the government of the country, which has traditionally been the business of men and not their responsibility. But as citizens on an equal footing with men, however, women cannot be indifferent to the political process that inevitably affects their everyday life.

Politics has indeed been men's business in the past but every woman now has the chance to change that situation. The conditions have to be created in which there will be a sufficient number of women in decision making position as well as in politics, to make gender an unremarkable attribute and the chances of women for higher positions would be inevitable and normal. Such conditionals would start with a change in attitude, both of men and women, towards the traditional sex roles in general and to the political participation of women in particular. An attitudinal change ties with a decrease or elimination of discriminatory practices in education, both formal and informal. Employment and adequate support systems are other two necessities for above change.

An increase in numbers of women, leading eventually to a gender balance, should permit women to break the difficulties of group dynamics that categorise pressure and potentially assimilate and silence them. Balanced numbers would produce changes in male perceptions and behaviour, as well as strengthen coalitions with others across the sex lines. Empirical research shows that an increased number of women at decision making level also affects women's perception and interests. Solidarity of women in politics could therefore be won by a substantial increase of their representation in legislature.

TYPE OF MINISTRIES WHERE WOMEN HOLD KEY-POSTS

Table 5 reveals the distribution of women by type of Ministry or decision making posts held by women. It illustrates the tendencies for women to be more easily accommodated in the social area. Except once, no one has given Cabinet rank. All are allotted either state or deputy ministerial berths which has hardly any decisive roles.

TABLE – 5

Shows the list of lady ministers of the Orissa Legislative Assembly, 1937-1995

Sl. No.	*Assembly and Name of the Members*	*Port Folio*	*Period of Ministership*
	FIRST ASSEMBLY—1952		
1.	Smt. Basanta Manjari Devi	Deputy Minister of Health	20-02-1952 to 19-10-19956
	SECOND ASSEMBLY—1957		
2.	Smt. Basanta Manjari Devi	Minister of Health (Excluding Local Self-Government and Relief and Rehabilitation)	06-04-1957 to 22-05-1959
	THIRD ASSEMBLY—1961		
3.	Smt. Saraswati Pradhan	Deputy Minister of Education	02-10-1963 to 08-03-1967
	FIFTH ASSEMBLY—1971		
4.	Smt. Nandini Satpathy	Chief Minister and Minister of Home, Political Services (Excluding Parliamentary Affairs) and Rural Development	14-06-1972 to 03-03-1973
	SIXTH ASSEMBLY—1974		
5.	Smt. Nandini Satpathy	Chief Minister and Minister of Home, Political Services	06-03-1974 to 03-04-1977

		Planning and Co-ordination, Industries	
	EIGHTH ASSEMBLY—1980		
6.	Smt. Saraswati Hembram	Deputy Minister of Community Development and Rural Reconstruction	09-06-1980 to 09-03-1985
	NINTH ASSEMBLY—1980		
7.	Kumari Frida Topna	* State Minister of Fisheries and Animal Husbandary, Education Sports & Youth Services.	10-03-1985 to 07-12-1989
		* State Minister of Education and Youth Services.	07-12-1989 to 03-03-1990
8.	Smt. Parama Pujari	* Deputy Minister of Harijan & Tribal Welfare	22-07-1986 to 07-12-1989
		* Health & Family Welfare	07-12-1986 to 03-03-1989
9.	Smt. Saraswatiu Hembram	* Deputy Minister of Community Development & Rural Reconstruction	22-07-1986 to 07-12-1989
		* State Minister of Community Development and Rural Reconstruction	07-12-1989 to 03-03-1990
	TENTH ASSEMBLY—1990		
10.	Dr. (Smt.) Kamala Das	State Minister of Education (Primary & Adult Education)	24-07-1990 to 10-03-1995
	ELEVENTH ASSEMBLY—1995		
11.	Smt. Bijayalaxmi Sahu	State Minister for Women and Child Development	10-03-1995 to continuing

Such positions should not be confined to social issues. All areas of politics affect women and in order for them to become effective agents of change, it is critical that women should be present in sufficient numbers in all policy making organs, especially in economic and political sectors which has till now remained predominantly the seat of males.

There are only the names of two women representatives from Orissa to Lok Sabha since 1937 to 1990; which speaks a very poor representation. They have not taken any key post there also. Similar in the case of Rajya Sabha, five ladies from Orissa were represented between 1937 to 1990. No one of them were given either any ministerial position or any important committee position except in two dormant area of petitions and library committee.

SOME INSIGHTS

The political inroads to decision making positions usually leads through the parliamentary system via political parties, trade unions etc. It has been found that, to a certain extent, the lack of women in the political foreground is due to their scarcity within those organs.

Even where parties, unions or associations have a relatively high percentage of female members; they are for their parent's or husband's socioeconomic and political elevated positions in society. It is not a result of their indigenous striving to make their political career as self-made one.

If women are in the top echelons of any mass organisations; their number is comparatively low. For this reason, the number of female representation in state and national machinery is invisible.

Where women have achieved power in politics they have made no difference, it has to be noted that these are individual women in male domain. At present, women live with the result of the policies made by men even if she occupies the apex position. If political responsibilities were shared equally between women and men, an additional capacity for shouldering these responsibilities would be made available. Major obstacles for women to be represented lies in unequal division of household and child-care duties. It hinders particularly the participation of women in political life, because it needs much investment of time for a better career in politics. Women's double burden, combined with the long and non-flexible time requirements of parties and parliament, prevent many women from becoming active in politics. Second obstacle is the prevailing negative attitudes towards women's movement, exposure, and above all participation in public life. Lack of healthy and democratic tradition, will power and confidence both on the part of candidate and electorate are also serious negative factors for women's active participation in politics.

Limited political knowledge, skill, and tactics in dealing political strategies are other handicaps for women's low ranking in representation. Understanding politics or not does depend very much on their structural position. It is also seen that less skilled (politically) women are used by political parties as their candidate for a silent support in their decision. We find not a single MLAs or MPs of Orissa are from any Lawyers, lecturers, journalists or Doctor's groups.

SOME SUGGESTIONS

1. Some fixed percentage of seats in Legislature, Parties and mass organisations should be reserved for women.
2. All high level posts should have at least one female candidate.
3. Special recruitment campaign for women in mass organisations and parties.
4. For political participation, education is a must. Girls should be encouraged in non-traditional areas of training and education which pertains to political

participation. The promotion research project, scholarship, seminars, community working, artistic activities, media should be sensitized on women's subjugation. Review of text-books and school manuals should be done to eliminate sexist bias from vocabulary and content.

5. Information through media should be sharp to cross out the subtle forms of discrimination experienced by women in public life. Publications should be made on role of woman in promotion of justice, peace and human rights.

CONCLUSION

To achieve a decisive role in politics, women have to become aware of power and their interest. Accordingly, women must be convinced that there can be no better advocates of their interests than themselves. It would surely make a difference in polity as well as in society.

REFERENCES

Catharie, A. Mackinnon, 1982, *Feminism, Marxism, Method and the State,* Sign, Spring

Chatterji, Shoma, 1989, *The Women's Search for an Identify,* Vikas Publications, New Delhi.

Committee on the States of Women in India, 1975, *Report,* "Towards Equality".

Friedan, B., 1965, *The Feminine Mystique,* Harmondswoth, Pengium.

Government of Orissa, *Council of Ministry,* (1937-90)

Morgan, D.H.J., 1985, *The Family, Politics and Social Theory,* Routledge and Kagan Paul Publications, U.S.A.

Patricia, Caplan, 1985, *Class and Gender in India,* Tavistook Publishers, Lndon.

Seminar *Reports* on Political Participation, Public Life, Women Decision-Making of UN Office at Vienna, 1990, 1991, 1992.

women participated on a much larger scale than in the non-cooperation movement. After Gandhi was arrested, Sarojini Naidu directed the Salt Satyagraha until her own arrest. Picketing was declared unlawful by the government and much attention was focussed on the arrested and lathi-charged women satyagrahis.[15]

There were several elections held in the second stage of the women's suffrage campaign. Although women's turnout increased over the period, the women's organisations themselves did not play a decisive role in electoral mobilisation, as they lacked the necessary organisational structure.

In the 1937 elections to Provincial Legislatures ... of the ... electorate ... women ... approximately 10 percent of the ... adult females were enfranchised. As a result of the 1937 elections, 56 women entered the legislatures. There were ... seats reserved for women in the provincial legislative assemblies, 10 women won ... and ... were nominated to provincial legislative councils. ... women who won were Congress candidates. None of the leaders of equal rights factions contested the elections.

INDICATORS OF RESPONSE OF FORMAL POLITICAL INSTITUTIONS TO WOMEN'S EQUALITY

The Committee on the Status of Women in India (CSWI) made an assessment of response by political parties and the electoral process to the principle of sex equality. Starting with the Constituent Assembly leaders of all political parties accepted the principle of sex equality without any debate or objection.

Studies commissioned by the CSWI concluded that in reality no party had recognised women as a source of political support.[14] This view can be supported by an examination of

16

WOMEN'S PARTICIPATION IN ELECTORAL POLITICS: A STUDY OF THE DHENKANAL ASSEMBLY CONSTITUENCY OF ORISSA

Mrs. Mandakini Das

The literacy rate among women in Dhenkanal is just half of the male literacy (As per 1991 Census). But the Assembly Constituency almost supports always to a lady candidate in every general election, which can be seen in the following analysis. In this paper, a discussion is made on the role of women in politics with special reference to electoral politics in Dhenkanal Assembly Constituency of Orissa.

I

Political participation connotes the extent to which citizens avail themselves of those ordinary democratic rights of political activity to which they are constitutionally entitled. It speaks of a citizenry always active and vigilant, possessing commitment to avail themselves of all the democratic political rights that are due to them. Availing of the rights being their main concern, such a citizenry tend to equip themselves in such a way that they would be able to avail all their rights. They also become conscious of and sensitive to the problems of political society and throw their weight in favour of strengthening the system facilitating participatory processes.

What political participation refers to is the process through which a segment of the citizenry strives to get its due shape from the society and polity by taking part in the political process in general and decision-making in particular. Political participation however does not necessarily carry the implication of ultimate decision-making power. The ultimate decision-making and law creating functions are handled by a small body of elected representatives.

Political participation may take different forms and be manifest in different methods. However, for the purpose of the present paper, the term is used to express participation of the women of Dhenkanal in the electoral process, particularly as candidates in the elections held to the Orissa Legislative Assembly since 1952. The selection of the women candidate of Dhenkanal is guided by the considerations that

(a) Dhenkanal represents a good combination of the culture of the coastal and highland Orissa;
(b) being a former feudatory state, it also resembles the other feudatory states which merged in Orissa in January 1948; and
(c) one of the most important women leaders of Orissa (Mrs. Nandini Satapathy) represented a constituency of the Dhenkanal District.

II

Dhenkanal is a land locked district situated at the heart of the State. It is bound by Cuttack, Puri, Phulbani, Bolangir, Sambalpur, Sundergarh and Keonjhar districts. Mahanadi, the largest river of Orissa is flowing in the border and Brahmani is flowing in the middle of the district. The Eastern Ghats is passing through this district.

However, this district is now divided into two, Dhenkanal and Angul districts. For our present purpose, we will analyse it as a single undivided district. As per the 1991 Census, the total population of the district is 1,900,675, out of which females are 926,532. It is mostly a district of villages where 1,712,661 people live. Out of total population, the Scheduled Castes (SC) are 313,574 and Scheduled Tribes (ST) are 232,514 which together constitute 31.88% of the total population of the district.

Dhenkanal is a large producer of coal which covers 7,377 hectors as compared with the total mineral area of 9,377 hectres as compared with the total mineral area of 9,053 hectors. The biggest colliery of Orissa is situated at Talcher. Besides coal, chromite covers 1,083 hector, graphite 102 hector, fire clay 408 hector and quartz and felspar 8 hectors area. In these mines, 8,741 workers are employed from which coal mines employee constitute 7,541 workers. (1990 Report). Out of the total geographical area of 1,092,000 hector the Forest area covers 491,000 hector which is 42.2% of the total area. (Report of 1989-90). The agricultural area of the district is 42.49%.

Due to the large deposit of coal, a thermal power station is already situated at Talcher and the construction of National Thermal Power Centre is going on in Kanihan of the district. The district is industrially coming up very fast. As an industrial belt in Talcher there is a Heavy Water Factory and Fertilizer Plant. At Angul, the largest Aluminium Factory of India (NALCO) is established. Besides these large industries, the medium size industries (like the Utkal Asbestos, Orissa Synthetics, Ipitata Refractories and Ipisteel) are coming up. There are 52 registered factories and 232 small scale Industrial Units in Dhenkanal which provide employment to 6,870 people (1987-88).

Dhenkanal has very inadequate means of transport in relation to agricultural, mineral, forest and industrial resources. Railway facilities are limited, road facilities too are inadequate. The inadequacy of transport facilities, hinders faster industrialisation. National Highways cover only 250.40 Kms.

While Major District Roads are 364.50 Kms. And other District Roads are of 267.51 Kms (1989-90).

As per the 1991 Census Report, the literate persons in the district are 847,257, which is 44.58% of the total population. 558,358 males are literates, the number of females is only 288,904, which is almost half of male literacy rate. In 1988-89, there were 2,282 Schools in primary stage, 562 at middle stage and 283 at secondary stage. But the number of Colleges is increasing largely. While there are three women's Colleges of degree level, the district is lucky to have one of the women Polytechnic Schools.

III

Election is an inevitable phenomenon in a democracy. It creates among the citizens a sense of involvement and participation in public affairs. Through exercise of this power of electoral decision-making, people exercise control over government and the broad outlines of public policy pursued by it. It is said that in a democratic government the right of decision-making belongs to the majority, but the right of representation belongs to all.

Since independence, ten General Elections (1952-1990) were held in Orissa on the basis of universal adult franchise. After the General Election of 1952 and 1957, there was a mid-term elections to the State Legislative Assembly in June 1961. The next General Election to the Assembly should have been held in 1966. But the next nation-wide Parliamentary election was held in February-March 1967. Since the interval of the Assembly Election and parliamentary Election would have been a small span of about six months, considering the unnecessary expenditure and administrative problems inherent in two consecutive elections, Parliament had extended the terms of Orissa Legislative Assembly till the 1st March 1967. This extension enabled the elections to the Legislative Assembly to be held simultaneously with the nation-wide General Elections in 1967.

The Fourth-General Elections to the Assembly having been held in the year 1967, the Fifth-General Elections would have been held in the year 1972. But following the Kendu leaves scandal, the Swatantra-Janacongress coalition government collapsed on 9th January 1971 and the Orissa Legislative Assembly was dissolved on 11th January 1971. So the Election Commission synchronised the elections to the legislative Assembly with the parliamentary election in March 1971. With the pre-mature dissolution of the Orissa Legislative Assembly in March 1973, the sixth Assembly Election was held in February 1974. In the Lok Sabha Election of 1977, people had cast their votes against the black period of emergency. The Janata Government at the centre decided to hold fresh Assembly Elections in nine states including Orissa in 1977. Thus elections to the Orissa Legislative Assembly were held in January 1977.

After this, due to intra-party conflict the pre-mature fall of Janata Ministry both in the centre and in Orissa took place for which Eighth Assembly Election was held in June 1980. The Ninth and Tenth General Electronics were held respectively in 1985 and 1990 followed by a bye-election in 1993 in the Hindol Constituency of Dhenkanal District.

An analysis of the candidates elected to the Legislative Assembly shows that Dhenkanal Constituency in particular and Dhenkanal district in general have sent more women representatives to it compared to other constituencies of Orissa. The only lady Chief Minister of Orissa Mrs. Nandini Satapathy was elected from Dhenkanal and known no defeat here, in her political career.

Rajmata Ratnaprave Devi was elected to the Legislative Assembly as a Genatantra Parishad candidate from Kamakshyanagar in 1957. She was also elected from Dhenkanal Constituency as a Genatantra Parishad candidate in 1961 and as a Swatantra candidate in 1967.

Entering the Orissa Assembly first, in October 1972,.Smt. Nandini Satapathy created a record of being elected five times consecutively. In 1974, she was elected from Dhenkanal as congress candidate defeating her nearest rival Swatantra candidate Raja Kamakshya Prasad Singhdeo Mahindra Bahadur. In 1974, Smt. Nalini Kumari Pattnaik had contested from Angul as Jana-Congress candidate. But she was defeated miserably.

In 1977, from Dhenkanal, Smt. Nandini Satapathy contested as a Janata candidate and in this election, she had no support of the Janata party in Orissa. On the other hand the eminent Janata Leaders of Orissa including Biju Pattnaik and Nilamani Routray displayed open political hostility to Nandini Satapathy at the time of election. Smt. Malati Chowdhury, wife of the former Chief Minister of Orissa (Sj. Nabakrishna Chowdhury) and a very highly respected social and political worker of Orissa became the main electoral opponent. Most of the Janata Leaders had their support for Malati Chowdhury as against Nandini Satapathy. Yet Nandini Satapathy won the elections to the Orissa Legislative Assembly in June 1977.

In 1980, Smt. Satapthy was elected from Dhenkanal as Congress(U) candidate where as in 1985 the same constituency elected her on Congress(I) ticket.

In 1990 Smt. Satapathy was elected to Assembly from Gandia Constituency, leaving Dhenkanal constituency to her son (Tathhagata Satapathy) to be elected as Janata candidate. Smt. Golapi Behera managed to get Janata ticket from Talcher due to her husband Sri Bhajamana Behera, the then Union Minister.

In the bye-election of Hindol held in 1993 due to the death of Sri Trinath Nayak, his wife Pata Nayak was elected from constituency reserved for the Scheduled Castes.

IV

With the exception of the elections of 1952 and 1971, in all other elections, women candidates have contested from Dhenkanal District. General Elections on the basis of universal adult franchise were held in India for the first time in 1952. In a backward district like Dhenkanal perhaps no lady had made up her mind to participate in this electoral politics.

The election of 1971 to the Orissa Legislative Assembly may be said to be a milestone in as much as it marked the end of leadership of one women leader, (Rajamata Ratnaprava Devi) and beginning of another (Smt. Nandini Satapathy) who started representing Dhenkanal constituency with effect from the next election held in 1974. Moreover in this Assembly Election of 1971, the performance of women candidates was worst in Orissa. Out of twelve lady contestants, only one was able to win the election and eight of them even forfeited their deposits.

So long as Rajmata Ratnaprave Devi contested from Dhenkanal as an opposition candidate, Congress was not able to have a foothold there, Despite all previous unpopular policies of the Dhenkanal ruling family, she was elected in all elections in which she was a candidate.

Regardless of whether Rajmata Ratnaprava Devi was a good candidate or not, the people of this former feudatory state, probable, voted for their erstwhile queen or the mother of the subsequent rule. The charisma that Ratnaprava Devi represented was not a cultivated charisma, it was ascriptive. The people for whom ascription being so honoured was enhanced by poverty, backwardness and lack of education of the people of their feudatory state. Such loyalty to the royal family however, was changed in 1974 when sri K.P. Singhdeo as a Swatantra candidate was defeated by Smt. Satapathy, Congress laid its strongholds in Dhenkanal, as a result even Sri Singhdeo had to change his affiliation to this party. Nandini

Satapathy replacing the Dhenkanal ruling house may be significant and indicative of a new socio-economic and cultural change in Dhenkanal.

In the Assembly Elections of 1974, Smt. Satapathy chose Dhenkanal as her constituency where she was able to be elected. Voters had responded positively to her appeal as "daughter-in-law of the soil". In consequent elections, her political training, financial and organisational support of the party nominating her, had smoothed the victory. Even the change of party colour and constituency did not have any negative impact upon the voters. The election of 1990 show how she managed to get her son elected from Dhenkanal as a Janata candidate, while she was elected as a Congress candidate from the nearby constituency Gondia.

In 1977, the defeat of Sarvodaya Leader, Smt. Malati Chowdhury was possible due to three reasons. Firstly, despite the controversial role during her Chief Ministership, Smt. Nandini Satpathy managed to change her party affiliation. She was able to get a Janata ticket to contest from Dhenkanal, even though some important Janata leaders had protested her nomination. The "Janata Wave" enabled her to be victorious. This election also proved how Smt. Satpathy is capable enough to measure rightly the pulse of the mass. Secondly, Smt. Malati Chowdhury was not able to get any party ticket. So the financial and organisational help of a party is not available to her. In terms of election propaganda she was far behind of Smt. Satpathy. Thirdly, the voters of Dhenkanal seems of not having any ideological orientation. Personality plays a dominating role in deciding the choice of the voters.

In 1990, Smt. Golapi Behera managed to get the Janata ticket due to her husband's influence. She was not having any political training, as a resuit, despite the "Janata Wave" she was defeated in Talcher.

In 1993 bye-election in Hindol, the untimely death of her husband enabled Smt. Pata Nayak to get the sympathy vote. Again, her victory was possible also due to the support of female voters for whom Orissa Chief Minister has taken various favourable decisions only after 1990.

To conclude, it may be said that women's participation as candidates in the electoral politics is on an increase. But the study shows that a woman candidate wins the election, if she gets the party support. It is very difficult for the women candidate to win the election as independent candidate.

17

WOMEN'S MOVEMENT: A CRAVE FOR GENDER EQUALITY

Dr.(Mrs.) Sharada Rath
Mrs. Jyotirmati Samantaray

Movements for women's equality all over the world have always been rooted within or have been the results of movements for democratic rights, people's rights, human rights and basic equality for human beings. Whether you take eighteenth or nineteenth century Europe or you take twentieth century Asia, Africa or Latin America, the trend is the same everywhere. (M. Krishnaraj, p.24).

'Feminist Movement' and 'Women's Movement' are terms which are frequently used interchangeably, although they represent different characteristics of the women's struggle. A feminist movement is founded primarily on the demand by women for equal rights and opportunities with men. The American feminist movement, for example, was based on a demand for equal social, political and economic opportunities with men. In India, the social reform movement of the 19th century, women's participation in national politics and Gandhiji's efforts to foster an ideology which restored their just and honoured position in society can be explained as the movement for women's emancipation. (Vijay Agnew).

Theorists on feminism classifies women's movements into two types, namely, women's equality movement and women's liberation movement. Women's equality movement aims at abolishing the most exploitative characteristics of feudal patriarchy and to put an end to the gender-based stratification system where women are forced to remain at the lowest rung of the social ladder, but women's liberation movement advocates an absolute freedom for the women and seems as an expression of extreme feminism, otherwise known as "radical feminism". (Vicky Randall, 1987). In sum, "women's uplift" can be seen as a corporate feminist ideology, while "equal rights" can be seen as a liberal feminist ideology. Corporate feminism is an ideology based upon the claims of a larger share for women in development, on the ground that as women, they have a special contribution to make. Liberal feminism proclaims that the rights of men should be extended to women on the ground that women are equal to men and thus should have the same rights. Any kind of women's movement fall into one or the other of these ideologies.

The question arises : What are the causes for the emergence of women's movement in different societies ? A commonsense view is that social changes are responsible for creating several claims, interests and demands even in case of women. But, specifically speaking, it may be mentioned that structural changes in the society which enable the middle class women in particular to redefine their role because of their education, skill, as well as exposure are responsible for the emergence of women's movements. Sometimes, women's movements take the form because of the contradictions women face in performing their actual roles. On the one hand, women have their domestic and reproductive roles, on the other, they are active citizens of the society. However, these roles of women in society are not properly recognised and the women are treated as 'inferior', 'subordinate', and 'worthless' creatures and they are being tortured like anything in society. When women become conscious of this fact, they revolt against these nasty social taboos, customs and traditions. They demand for equality, justice, rights and identities through movements, revolt and resistance. The autonomous women's groups which emerged in the 70's have challenged the Marxist paradigm that sees women's movement as inseparable from working class movement and autonomous women's groups are seen as a threat to the unity of the working class struggle. There is also a growing criticism of the "development paradigm" which overlooks the various dimensions of women's issues.

WOMEN'S MOVEMENTS IN DIFFERENT COUNTRIES

Political theorists have now accepted that movements, protests and struggles are legitimate expressions of political behaviour and the meaningful explanation of political participation of individuals. Hence, a number of theories have developed using the causes, issues and methods of women's movements as well as various organisations involved in these movements. (Guida and Rhode, 1990). What needs to be emphasised here is that in each country the movement adopted itself to the history of culture and politics of its own society. (Kiran Devendra, 1994). Therefore, it is necessary to mention here women's movements for gender equity in different countries.

Women's movement in Great Britain originated during 1840 to 1870 and the middle class women. The objective of these movements was mainly ethical concentrating on the demand for gender equality as a part of moral reforms. Then, the movement was directed towards the social reforms of the society through legal changes. Women's movements in Britain , through different periods of history can be divided into four phases. In the first phase of the movements (1840-1870), women organisations were formed on wide variety of issues like equality in the social sphere, equality of opportunities in case of employment, equality in case of charity etc. The second phase of the movement (1871-1920) was dominated by the issue of constitutional right like women's suffrage. Women's organisations focussed entirely on the demand for franchise right, one of such organisations was National Union of Women's Suffrage Society (NUWSS). The third period of the movement (1905-1918) focussed on the demand for right to vote but adopted militant tactics generating much publicity. The fourth stage of the British women's movement was again dominated by women's organisations which continued as the National Union of Societies for Equal Citizenship (NUSEC) and pressed for constitutional equality of sexes under the law. These organisations also demanded for certain legislative relief for women and finally these movements succeeded in 1928 by obtaining equal political rights of women. (J.K.Chopra, 1993).

Likewise, the women's movement in the United States of America can be put into four stages and it was started little earlier than that of Great Britain. During the first stage of the movement (1820-1866), there were no permanent organisations devoted specifically to the demands of women's rights. The Declaration of Independence in 1776 declared that "all men are created equally" and intentionally / unintentionally left out women to enjoy equality. In 1848, Mort and Stanton organised the first women's rights convention in Seneca Falls, New York and made a declaration, "We hold these truths to be self-evident that all men and women are created equal...." However, the movement for women's rights got a setback during the Civil War. During the second stage of the women's movement in America (1866-1890), permanent organisations with specific aims and objectives were formed like the National Women Suffrage Association. During this period, the 14th Amendment was added to the Constitution and was regarded as a milestone on the path of equality in the United States. But, the Amendment failed to extend specific guarantees to women. Rather it used the word "male" and not "female" to identify citizens of America for the purpose of elections to different political offices of the country. Feminist Elizabeth Cady Stanton had rightly predicted in 1866 that "if the word 'male' be inserted in this amendment it will take a century to get it out again". Section 1 of Amendment XV to the Constitution, ratified on 30 March 1870 reads : "The rights of citizens of the United States to vote shall not be denied or abridged by the United States or by any state on account of race, color, or previous condition of servitude". This Article also does not include "sex" in order not to give equal political rights to women. The third stage of the movement started from 1890 and continued upto 1920. During this period, the National Women Suffrage Association protested the fifteenth amendment and advocated that women's suffrage was a means to achieve major improvements in the economic and social situation of the women in the United States. Finally, in 1920, the 19th Amendment was ratified and became a part of the Constitution and thereby women got the franchise right. The fourth stage of the movement started in post-1920 period and continues even today for obtaining not only equal political right, but to obtain equality of women in all spheres of life. To guarantee equal rights to women, another attempt was made to include the Equal Rights Amendment (ERA), the proposed 27th Amendment to the Constitution. ERA was first introduced in Congress in 1923 by leaders of the National Women's Party who felt that getting the right to vote would not be enough to change women's status. But it took nearly half a century to be passed in Congress in 1972. However, in 1982, the ERA could not be passed and died out as it could not get the support of required states for amendment. Although ERA could not be enacted, several efforts were made by the federal government to eliminate sex-discrimination in the labor market. The 'Affirmative Action" was used to implement the policy of non-discrimination in employment by the federal government and its contractors. At the same time, the issue of equal pay to comparable work obtained national attention during a strike of female municipal workers in San Jose, California, in 1981, even if The Equal Pay Act was in implementation since 1979.

Analysing the role of women in a Muslim dominated country like Algeria, it has been found that women's movement there is seriously discouraged because, women's role in the development of the country has not been properly recognised. However, historical evidence shows their active participation in the freedom struggle of the country. Even if the women in this country strictly adhere to *Purdha* system, their "under life" was strong, for example, Djamila Bouhired and Djamila Boupacha were the more articulate representatives of thousands of women terrorists who worked for the success of the Algerian revolution. They identified themselves totally with the liberation movement and proved that they were as tough as male persons. However, after the success of the Algerian revolution, the women's movement had got a set back. Women returned back to their homes and remained confined to their domestic chores. Their contribution to the success of the revolution was not recognised and women were again made to feel that they were no longer needed by their countrymen.

WOMEN'S MOVEMENT IN INDIA

Women's movement in India proves itself as unique compared to the similar movements in other countries. First, the movement began much before the country became independent in 1947. Secondly, India had produced a number of social reformers and political leaders who were very much concerned about the low status of women particularly in the 18th and 19th centuries. Almost all the socio-religious movements during that period aimed at creating and mobilising public opinion in favour of elevating women's status in society. In other countries, while the main concern was to give political rights to women, in India, the main objective was women's social uplift, as for centuries together, women in India suffered from low social status because of the prevailing social customs and taboos.

Women's movement in India had adopted two types of ideologies or approaches, so far as improvement of the women's plight was concerned. One was "women's uplift" in order to enable the women to play a more constructive role in the society by reforming social practices, and the other was to provide equal rights for men and women, that is, the extension of civil rights enjoyed by men to women in the political, economic, and social spheres.

ISSUES OF WOMEN'S MOVEMENT IN INDIA

The debate on women's role and participation in popular movements has raised several questions regarding organisational and leadership issues, nature of struggle, mobilising mechanisms and strategies, perspectives on micro issues in relation to larger political process and ideological dimensions. However, in India, the lack of historical dimension in the analysis of women's position in different movements creates difficulties for the researcher in understanding the emergence and growth of ideology of women's movement and its relationship with the National Movement at the macro level and the social movements at the micro level.

During pre-independence period, main issues of women's movement were to provide social equality to women by emancipating them from evil social customs and traditions. But, after independence, the issues changed and all the women's movements spoke for the economic uplift of women through eradication of poverty, education, creation of awareness, and creating jobs for women. Thereafter, the women issues took a new turn by putting emphasis upon empowerment of women through participation in decision - making bodies.

Participation of women in social and political processes is understood by some scholars as organisational. Some scholars suggest that a genuine mass - based women's movement can grow out of the grass-root participatory organisation of women. (Kumud Sharma, 1987). It has been held that the grassroots organisations of urban and rural poor women are vital instruments to provide them collective strength, bargaining capacity and collective articulation of their interests. (N.K. Banerjee, 1995). Since independence, national development strategies under different plans and programmes have promoted women's grass-root organisations like Mahila Mandals etc. for the delivery of services to women or for creating income-generating activities for women. The structure, effectiveness and perspectives of these organisations varied from state to state. Several reviews and evaluations of Mahila Mandals have commented on the non-representative character, vagueness of objectives, lack of resources and poor performance of these organisations. (Kumud Sharma, 1992).

The question arises : Do women's issues get exposed through women's participation in broader movements ? It is ,in fact, widely recognised that while women become active in militant struggle for not only women's cause, but for a common cause, the issues of women's oppression and suppression within the family and society do not get automatic expression as the issues of the movement. In such broader movements, women's issues are relegated to the background as it had happened in case of national movement for independence or the environmental protection movement of today.

Leela Kasturi, in her Occasional Paper No. 25 (1995) explains the various aspects of women's status in India and points out the related gender issues. She has analysed three seminal documents which span a period of fifty years (1940 - 92) and divides the women's movement in India into three phases, namely, movement of pre-independence period, of post-independence period and the movement of post-1975 period. The first is the Report of the Subcommittee on "Women's Role in Planned Economy " (1947), the second is

the Report of the Committee on the Status of Women (1974), and the third is the National Perspective Plan for Women, 1988.

The contents of these three reports reflect the issues of women's movements and the extent and the method in which women leaders tried to articulate the women's issues. All these reports pointed out that though there was perceptible change in the status of women in India, it is not uniform for all women in Indian society. Inequality is found even among women themselves. (Leela Kasturi, 1995).

WOMEN'S MOVEMENTS IN INDIA: VARIOUS DIMENSIONS

Participating in both the national and women's movement, elite women campaigned for social legislations in the fields of education, health, economy and social equality for women. The movement started with the major issues of marriage, adoption, abolition of Sati and property rights of women. To their credit , it may be said that, the national leaders including women leaders highlighted the socio-economic phenomena which put the bottlenecks on the progress of Indian women.

In the next phase, the women's movement in India demanded equality of sexes. However, Art.15(3) empowers the state to introduce special measures for the protection of women and children irrespective of its obligation not to discriminate on the grounds of sex. (Basu, 1990). In spite of the constitutional provisions for gender equality as well as special privileges for women, women's equality particularly, in economic and social spheres remained as a day dream for a long time. Though the Report of the Subcommittee on "Women's Role in Planned Economy" (1947) outlined a proposal for the realisation of women's equality, it was not retained as a guide for which, the question of women's uplift remained as only a political agenda till 1956 without any constructive action taken thereupon. Till mid-seventies, women leaders were unable to evolve their own platforms for identifying, projecting and focussing their own issues due to the absence of an energetic and forceful women's movement (S. Rath, 1996).

In the 60's, as a response to the failure of national level organisations and political parties to take up women's problems as issues in their agenda, many action groups relating to women's issues emerged at local levels as well as at national level. These groups drew attention of the public to the nature of social transformation and mobilised public opinion to protest on issues which they thought as against their larger interests.

We may cite here certain movements of the later part of this century when women in India became conscious of their own problems and led the movement for their social, economic and political uplift. For example, women's participation in the prohibition movement in Garhwal in the sixties is significant in bringing out the leadership potential among the women. In like manner, during the same period, a Sarvodaya leader Sunderlal Bahuguna and his wife initiated resistance against the growing menace of alcholism at Ghansali in the Tehri district. Sarala Behn, a Gandhian worker, who became successful in activising women power in Uttarakhand through her organisation at Kausani in Almora district found the possibilities of mobilising women against alcoholism. Tara Devi at Choma and Shyma Devi at Gopeswar also led women demonstrators against alcoholism. During this period, women leaders were also accepted by the community as social activists and elites having concern for the society as a whole. For example, Shyama Devi was a lady member of the Gopeswar Civil Committee which took a delegation to the District Magistrate at Almora to close a liquor shop which was selling liquor for the last thirty-five years. The Prohibition Movement which affects greatly the life of women in family,

in community and in society as a whole, brought out the attitude and perception of rebellion among these women.

The most recent phase of women's movement dates from around the mid-seventies. This was sparked off by the report of the Committee on the Status of Women which motivated women to form activist groups to articulate and put forth their demands as well as to fulfil their demands through social and legal actions. Mid-1970s saw the beginning of a fundamental shift from the domination of the modernisation paradigm of development thinking and intervention to a systematic search for alternatives. (P. Oakley, 1991).

The women's question as such and the commitment to eliminate gender disparities disappeared from the political agenda by all the political parties during the period of 1956 to 1975. The varied failures of women's movement strengthened the structure of patriarchy and the increased inequality and exploitation of women. However, the Committee on the Status of Women, for the first time in 1975, recommended several important measures for the eradication of gender inequality in every sphere - social, economic and political.

The appointment of the CSWI and the publication of its report took place in a period of political unrest. National Emergency was imposed in 1975 with great opposition from the people. During this period, there were several democratic people's movements, labour strikes, agrarian and student unrest, protests against food shortages, inflation, unemployment and corruption which ultimately culminated in the Total Revolution movement led by late Sri Jaya Prakash Narayan. (Bimal Prasad, 1992). In all these protest movements, women participated substantially, though for common cause and not for any women- specific issues. Once women were mobilised even for general causes, they began to realise women specific issues like atrocities against women, torture, rape etc. Hence, since 1977 onwards, women's protests on various issues gathered momentum without having halt at any stage.

General Elections of 1980 brought Mrs Indira Gandhi back to power. In the same year, seven national women's organisations presented a memorandum to the government. (Indian Women in the Eighties : Development Imperative), which influenced the Planning Commission's decision to include for the first time a chapter on "Women and Development" in the Sixth Five Year Plan document. Most of the recommendations were drawn on the approaches and analysis of the three official Working Groups mentioned above. This indicates the vigour and effectiveness of the women's movement which compelled the government to have a dialogue with the women's groups before making any women-related public policy. Again, in 1985 a National Convention was convened by some groups of women's organisations to review the developments of women's status in India.

In the post-1975 period women's organisations conscientised the wider society, worked with all classes of women. Combining developmental activities with mobilisation for socio-economic rights, these organisations put a limited but successful pressure on the state for legislative action to curb exploitation of women in matters relating to marriage, rape and worker's rights. Thus, while separate and isolated gender-based movement was regarded as essential to unify women vertically as well as horizontally, collaboration with other socio-economic and political movements was also seen nonetheless necessary. Therefore, the women's movement joined the Civil Rights movements and worker's movements. The women's movement challenged state policies on different issues like population, environment, planning, agriculture, rural development, education as well as women's employment, training and organisation of women workers and so on. Negatively also, the women's movements protested against

distorted portrayal of women on media. As a consequence of all these movements, the dimensions of women' movements became increasingly broad-based. Their concern has now shifted to such basic issues as the state of polity and economy, criminalisation and communalisation of politics, communalism per se and fundamentalism. Two events, namely, the case of Saha Bano and the self-immolation of a young widow, Roop Kanwar in Rajasthan brought the issue of fundamentalism and revivalism into the forefront of debate and discussion.

In 1987, the Central government appointed a Commission to study the problems of self-employed women and women employed in informal sectors. Thereafter, the government chalked out The National Perspective Plan for Women (NPP) which was an exercise on the part of the government exclusively ignoring the involvement of the women organisations in such an important task. At that time, there was a public statement that there should be a national debate on the Plan before it was adopted as a policy. When no response came from the government, seven national women's organisations invited a public debate in which thirty-nine organisations from different parts of the country participated. Their comments and suggestions were collected on the basis of which the document was published under the title "The National Perspective Plan for Women 1988-2000."

The NPP reviews women's condition in nine areas, namely, rural development and agriculture; employment and training; education, health and family welfare; legislation, media and communication; supportive services; political participation and decision-making and voluntary action. The NPP acknowledges the need to increase women's participation and representation in the political process and recommended for 30% reservation of seats for women in the legislatures. The Perspective Plan ,in short, appears to believe that by creating a few top structures and co-opting women in these decision-making bodies, a number of complex gender-related problems like, women's subordination, inequality in power, resources and active opposition from powerful and organised forces can be solved.

Moreover, during this period, the women's organisations, through their movements, demanded the implementation of the UN Convention on the Elimination of All Forms of Discrimination against Women. The women's movement also demanded the recognition of the right to work as a fundamental right. The other demand was for the establishment of statutory autonomous Commissions for women at the Centre as well as at the state levels as recommended by CSWI (1975). Accordingly, a Bill on National Commission for Women was introduced in 1989 and passed in 1990 and in 1992, the National Commission for Women was instituted at the centre and the several state governments created State Commissions for Women.

CONCLUSION

To conclude, it can be said that women's movement in India started to fight with evil customs and traditions which had created a patriarchal male-dominated society where women enjoyed a position of subordination and inequality. Then, it was found that male-bias thinking, planning and implementation of development programmes had affected women's position in the family, the community and in the society at large. Women were considered as inferior and became unequal in terms of benefits, entitlements, and allocation of resources. The question therefore, is not whether women should be integrated into development and existing structures, but whether the existing structures and strategies should be changed in order to benefit women.

It is now increasingly realised that the Indian state is not gender-neutral, as society and state are influenced by patriarchal values, and atrocities against women are being used as instruments of political action. The state's failure becomes evident when it fails to create real and reliable equity and equality for the female sex. Hence, women's movements are no more confined only with the gender equality, women's emancipation, development and empowerment but with such issues as fundamentalism, environmentalism, communalism and the state of polity and economy. As a result of all these movements, women now want to be associated not only with political processes but also with the formal political system and government.

REFERENCES

Agnew, Vijay, 1979, *Women in Indian Politics,* Shakti Books, Vikas Publishing House, New Delhi.

Banerjee, N.K.; 1995, "Grassroot Empowerment (1875-1990) : A Discussion Paper", *Occasional Paper* No. 22, Centre for Women's Development +Studies, New Delhi.

Basu, Aparna, 1976, "The Role of Women in Indian Struggle for Freedom", B.R. Nanda, (ed.) *Indian Women: From Purdah to Modernity,* Vikas, New Delhi.

Basu, Durga Das; 1990, *Introduction to the Constitution of India,* 13th ed. Prentice-Hall of India, pvt. Ltd.

Chopra, J.K. ; 1993, *Women in the Indian Parliament* (A Critical Study of Role), Mittal publications, New Delhi.

Devendra, Kiran; 1994, *Changing Status of Women in India,* Vikas, New Delhi.

Georgia, Ashworth; 1986, *Of Violence and Violation : Women and Human Rights,* London .

Guida, West and Blumberg Rhode (eds.); 1990, *Women and Social Protest,* New York, Oxford University Press.

Kasturi, Leela; 1995, "Development, Patriarchy, and Politics : Indian Women in the Political Process, 1947-1972", *Occasional Paper* No. 25, CWDS, New Delhi.

Krishnaraj, Maithreyi, (ed,) *Women's Studies in India, Some Perspectives,* Popular Prakashan Pvt. Ltd. Bombay

Oakley, Peteret. al.; 1991, *Projects with People : The Practice of Participation in Rural Development,* Oxford & IBH Publishing Co. Pvt. Ltd.

Prasad, Bimal; 1992, *Jaya Prakash Narayan,* Vikas, New Delhi.

Rath, Sharada, 1996, "Feminist Movement in India : Contemporary issues and Leadership", *Public Policy Research Newsletter,* Center for Governmental Services, Indiana State University, Terre Haute, Indiana, Winter, Vol. IV, No.2

Sharma, Kumud; 1987, "Women in Struggle : Role and Participation of Women in Chipko Movement in Uttarakhand Region of U.P.", *Occasional Paper*, Centre for Women's Development Studies, New Delhi.

Sharma, Kumud; 1991-92, "Grass-root Organisations and Women's Empowerment : Some Issues in the Contemporary Debate", *Shamya Shakti*, Vol. VI.

Stifling, Friedrich Ebert; 1993, *Women in Politics: Forms and Processes*, Har Anand Publications Pvt. Ltd. New Delhi.